# Relentlessly Resilient

## *Overcoming the Resistance*

Monique Johnson

This book is available for purchase online at Envision1t.com and with distributors nationwide.
Edited by Ericka Baldwin at ErickaEmends.com
Cover design by Graphiczstar

ISBN Paperback 978-1-7379807-0-4
ISBN eBook 978-1-7379807-1-1

# Praise for the Book

*Commendations, Praise, and Reflections from a Sanctified Psalmist*

*– Elder Niki Keys*

*"Biblically, it is written; let another man praise thee!*
*It is my esteem pleasure to share in a synthesis of the literary writ of a powerful woman of purpose. Relentlessly Resilient's finest -Monique Johnson is poised, business-oriented, anointed, and yes, relentlessly resilient. The chapters are timely portrayals of this destiny carrier!*

*After an attentive perusal of Monique's literary work, the following was ascertained and impactful from within chapter 17:*
*Monique, clearly and literally, paints a picture of the sustainability that can be fostered while navigating amongst struggle and determination! Parenthetically, her leading quote attests to the value of surviving the refiner's fire which yields a high value, individualistically. I would encourage one who is in the midst of a storm to pay attention to chapter 17 as a source of strength, a depiction of vulnerability, fortitude, and an expected end declaration because she saw (vision), recorded it, decreed and manifestation occurred! My takeaway from chapter 17, all things are possible if we have faith in God ✍️.*

*Chapter 20 summations. The very title alone draws you into the text. How insightful; "Taking those L's with Grace."*
*The word of God admonishes us to not even look like we are fasting when we consecrate! Thus, why can't we embrace loss and still navigate adversity and hardship like a worthy soldier? Chapter 20 engaged me by evidencing that it is possible to lose gracefully! Additionally, to be not weary in welldoing, for in due season…! Just as this great author had many ebbs and flows, faith in God has rendered her to become a modern-day example of the miraculous!*

*I strongly recommend this motivating read. Happy exploration and welcome to Resilience with Monique!"*

*Niki Keys h.c.*

*"This book is a book about healing, transformation, and giving people the voice to fight what they thought couldn't be defeated. The author has a way of addressing different areas where you can't help but see yourself reflected inside this book. Some way form or fashion. Your story is in this book, and your chapter to victory is in this book."*

**Josias Jean-Pierre, Amazon Best Seller, Author, & Motivational Speaker**

*"I find the author, Monique Johnson, true to her title in both chapters 5: Life with a Drug Addict & 6: Getting Past the Hurdles. She showed a dedicated and resilient side of her I never knew. She was relentless in her pursuit of a future, her career, and making a life for herself and her child. She did all this while trying to keep her love interest in check. Not an easy balance if you ask me. At the same time, dealing with a person with a drug problem, she was trying to grow herself as a woman. To deal with that takes a resilient person. To write about it, still be in her right mind, and not be afraid of drug dealers is one hell of a woman. She was dedicated to God and her family. I'm proud of you! This is a best seller."*

**Pops**

*"Monique Johnson is relentless and resilient. In her chapters, you will see how, after each knockdown, she kept standing on her faith in God. Chapter 18, Load Up We're Ready for Battle, prepares us for what's coming. Load up is the full armor of God. The author was on the battlefield fighting for her two sons. Because she was resilient and relentless and had God on her side, her sons were granted favor. They were given a second chance in life. In Chapter 20, Taking Those Ls with Grace, the author lets the reader know that it takes faith in God to keep us afloat. The closer our relationship with Jehovah, the faster and harder the fiery darts will be thrown our way; our faith is our shield of protection. Thank you for painting the picture of what faith looks like. To God be the glory! Thank you, Monique, for sharing your story."*

**A woman who walked a similar path; Mom**

# The Author's Why

I tell my story of the mother who cried for her son as she watched the bailiff take him away in handcuffs after the harsh sentence. I tell it for the father who did not realize the negative impact he'd leave on his child when he decided to let the mother raise him on her own. I tell it for the next generation, my grandsons and children yet to be born and yet to be heard. The story I share comes with a resolution on how to overcome the resistance. *This is why I tell it.*

What stories will the ears of future generations be inclined to hear? What legacy will be passed down through each household to ensure the next generation will be better than the last, to ensure the next generation knows who the true God is, and how the true God kept his hand upon the family that the next generation sprung from? What do we want our grandchildren to know that we should have known or could have known? How do we get that message to them, the next generation? *This is why I tell it.*

It is in our writing, it is in our stories on-screen and off-screen, it is in our blogs or social media posts, and it's in our YouTube videos where lessons can be shared, and healing can begin. A new wave of digital communication is taking our writing and voices to another level. The pen and ink days may be over, but communication will never stop. Communication can be written, drawn, painted in art, or communicated audibly through digital spaces. It is our responsibility to ensure we speak that which our Creator, the Most-High God, and our Lord and Savior Jesus the Christ wants to be communicated to generations. For this reason, I write, speak, document, and post. *This is why I tell it.*

# Dedication

I dedicate this book to my mother and my children. My mother is an amazing woman of faith and unconditional love. She demonstrates these characteristics in her daily life and does not accept negative talk from anyone. When doctors gave her a negative diagnosis over forty years ago, she did not accept it. Instead, she stood on the Word of God that says Jesus dealt with all sickness and disease at the cross. While my mom is my rock, my three children, whom God has allowed me to bring forth, are my motivation. These beautiful beings energize me, and I refuse to quit. I am *relentlessly resilient* for them.

# Contents

# Introduction

The morning I found myself sitting on a curb in an unfamiliar city was a significant turning point for me. I was almost done with my first year in college and looking forward to the next, but now I was facing a crossroads. I would soon embark on a journey I never thought I'd travel. This situation felt like a television drama, and I had the starring role. My role was that of a naïve eighteen-year-old, who was learning about herself, other people, and life. I was fresh out of high school, strong-willed, outspoken, cute, and having all of the ingredients of *that girl*. The girl all the boys wanted to talk to, but were not sure if she'd give them the time of day. I found that when younger boys did not know how to approach me, older men certainly would. I've always been more mature than most girls my age. I guess that is why I never dated guys my age. I was mature for my age yet still inexperienced in life. I had a know-it-all attitude, but knew nothing in the grand scheme of things. It is a shame that I had to hit the ground hard to realize I had much more growing to do. *Yet, even in my fall, I remained resilient.*

I went from struggle to struggle and from glory to glory in certain phases of my life. It was rough at times, but through my mom's example, I could turn off the negative thinking that could have held me back from breaking through. The amount of control I maintained over my thoughts made a difference in my ability to move forward. My mother moves through life with a "can do" attitude, so I know that is where I got the idea that I can do anything I set my mind to accomplish. I share this approach to life with my children, who have experienced moments of paralysis on their path to purpose at different points in their lives. My children have experienced disappointments and challenges from being raised in a single-parent household. My sons, intelligent, handsome, and humble individuals, have made bad decisions that landed them in the criminal justice system. It did not matter how nice of a neighborhood we lived in or how much I spent providing a private school education; both have had entanglements with the criminal justice system.

The nights I spent on my knees calling on God for His protection and deliverance did not go unanswered. Today, I am happy to say they have overcome the legal issues and are now navigating fatherhood. I can see pieces of my resilience in my sons, especially my eldest, Tyrell. He does not give up when things get hard. My younger son, Jamar, is still on his journey to figure out what he wants out of life, but he bounces back much quicker than before. My daughter, Kalani, is a boss in progress. She is strong-willed, free-spirited, kind, and humble but has bouts of anxiety. The more she observes me pray and overcome, the more she has begun to make moves to change her mindset. She is overcoming! She reminds me of my own words when I have moments of challenge. As parents, we bear the responsibility of ensuring we plant good seeds so that our children will have something to draw from when they encounter obstacles along their road to purpose. I understand the Proverb: "Train up a child in the way he should go, and when he is old, he will not depart from it." Proverbs 22:6 KJV. Key point: when he is old. Now that my sons are adults, I see how Relentlessly Resilient they are. From abandonment by male figureheads, fathers, and uncles to searching for their identity in the streets, these young men have risen out of ash piles when most would have been eaten alive.

*Relentless Resilience*, for me, is that bounce-back spirit inside a person that does not allow someone to stay down when they get knocked down. It is the ability to stand up again and thrive even after being held back by the resistance – that opposing force that wants to stop us from discovering who we are and what purpose we serve in the earth. It is a sad commentary when a person gives in to the resistance and quits believing they have a purpose. All of the talent and potential never gets shared. The light dims until it goes completely dark. I believe my purpose is to prevent you from allowing your light to go dim. I want you to know that you can change the bulb. Changing the bulb is changing your mindset so the light will continue to shine. Your resilience is required in the earth. Be relentless about it.

## Arise in Resilience

*A hard-knocks life is how the hard-headed learn.*
*It makes me wonder where is their ability to discern.*
*Naked truths and dressed-up lies. Why is truth the one they despise?*
*Is it because the alternative is not as sexy?*
*It showed up all exposed, with stuff hanging out looking all messy?*
*Yeah, I know, truth is ugly if it's been in hiding.*
*Under a rug or in a dumpster with lies and filth abiding.*
*Maybe it's none of this; instead, it's the feeling of bliss.*
*You get this when doing anything you want, and consequences you dismiss.*
*Street school, that's one hell of a campus where any and all situations arise.*
*You may walk through facilities of torment or cafés of exhilaration.*
*While you are taking it all in, don't miss the acceleration.*
*Your mind may become a victim of obliteration.*
*Do you think the streets are going to take it easy?*
*No, it's continually crying out, "you have to please me."*
*It's like you hopped onto a treadmill with speed levels too high.*
*You tried to keep up but weren't ready for this ride.*
*The folks you were following were going so fast.*
*You never took time to learn from their past.*
*They told you and showed you, but you didn't hear.*
*Your lack of spiritual discernment silenced your ear.*
*To the sounds and screams of everyone inside.*
*So, you, my friend, have been taken on a wild ride.*
*But if you noticed the hand that emerged in the passing shadow.*
*That was the hand of God trying to rescue you from dangers you didn't know.*
*Don't worry; He'll be right there waiting when you are ready to leave.*
*He'll give you mercy and grace for your failure to at first believe!*
*You came out of a bad situation, and you had zero notion*
*that after the battle, Resilience would be your portion.*

# Chapter 1

# Young and Dumb

*I thought I was the good one. I did what I was supposed to do. I helped and I encouraged. I never did it for likes. I did it because I wanted to love and encourage others; unfortunately, my kindness emitted vibes of availability and desire.*

**MJEnvisionit**

In love with a roughneck. Some of you know exactly what I am talking about. In the 1990s, it was 2 PAC or Treach from Naughty by Nature. In the early 2000s, it was Tyrese, Vin Diesel, or the gorgeous Paul Walker; may he rest in peace. It was the bad boys and hip hop for me. I vibed with the sounds of Digital Underground. I kicked it with my girls and bounced to the screaming lyrics of the rapper Mystikal; Danger! Watch Yourself! The Hip Hop era was like the rising of a phoenix with captivating energy of intrigue and sparked a fire in the music industry that has not gone out to this day. I am a product of that era. Rap videos painted a picture of what would have had our great-grandmothers clutching their pearls; and great-grandfathers taking their sons out to the woodshed for a wake-up call, if you know what I mean. This genre of music was bold, threatening, and, unfortunately truthful for some members of society. The glitz and glamour became all too enticing. So many of our young boys and men sought to be part of it. Where the boys went, the girls followed. They wanted to imitate the women they saw in the hip-hop scene with the handsome rapper on their arms. If she couldn't get the rapper, then she'd take the local bad boy.

It makes no sense, right? *Of course not!* How we think as teenagers is much different from how we think as mature adults. I look around at today's generation. I see young girls showing off their precious bodies, having babies for guys who only wanted them for a moment, and leaving with a child to raise. I ponder why they are doing this to themselves and the precious little lives they are creating? Is it impulse, excitement, a cry for help, or loneliness? No matter the answer, I want you to know that you can overcome any challenge. I remember when I was young. I was somewhat intrigued by the same type of guys, but luckily for me, I never let myself get in too deep with their lifestyle. I have always wanted a lot out of life. I've always dreamed of going to college and one day owning my own company or becoming a successful business manager. Besides, I had a beautiful, kind, supportive mother who poured so much love into me that I never wanted to intentionally disrespect her. I was mindful of choices and consequences, for the most part. Unfortunately, it was the bad boys for me. I loved the excitement. I enjoyed the music of the street culture. I'd get excited when a guy pulled up in his muscle car playing the latest hip hop jam with the volume turned up and the base vibrating. I was ready to party. Rappers like Doug E Fresh, Erick B and Rakim, and LL Cool J had us in constant dance mode. The images I saw on MTV or BET music videos showed guys with nice-looking bodies, exciting lifestyles, money, and what we call "swag" today. Hip-hop artists like these had the young ladies in my world wanting the tough guy with good looks and a cool-looking car.

Delon was that guy in my life. He had the looks but not the car. *I'll get into that later.* I met him on the bus. My little brother and I took the bus from our new school, near the beach community on the west side of Los Angeles. My mom transferred us out of our school district to obtain a better education. Also, we had been confronted by gang members who lived across the highway that divided our school from our home. We lived in what was known as the blue or crip territory and our school was in the red, or blood territory. We were not part of any gang, but we lived among them. I even dated a couple of guys from both gangs, but at different times. There was a time when I had to tell a guy I liked to run quickly across the highway when he left my porch because someone recognized him from the opposing gang. I did not have to worry about that with Delon because he was from the same gang but a different "set." Back then, a brother could get beat pretty bad or shot if someone from one of the gangs thought he was "set tripping" (basically disrespecting another gang member's neighborhood). I hated it when my brother and I would walk home from school, or get off of the bus nearby and have to pass the neighborhood bullies. Some knucklehead would shout out to him, asking what set he was from. Or they would say something disrespectful to me. I socked a guy for doing that to me in school. I was immediately suspended. I was a good student and on the honor roll. I just could not stand ignorance on display. I was quick to address it. Since my brother was never in the street life and was younger than me, I stood up for him. If anyone had something to say that could potentially get my brother drawn into a fight, I would jump in and try to shut it down. I would end up fighting or cursing someone out. It was all stupid, but was a very real part of my experience as a youth living in the urban center of Los Angeles.

I learned a lot about the dark side of the streets. It was a wild ride with Delon. We started so good. I was taken in because he was cute and played football for the local college. I had no idea about his bad-boy background until much later. The attraction was strong between us. Delon was handsome. He had an athletic physique, beautiful skin, and a face that should have been on the cover of a magazine. He was very social. People knew him from all over Los Angles and Compton. He said all of the right things to get me, and he got me. This brother had all kinds of girls after him, but he chose me. He enjoyed hanging out with me and took me around his family and friends. His grandmother and aunt loved me. They thought I was the best thing for Delon. I never knew how his mother felt because she was not usually around. She was recently remarried and focused on her younger children from this marriage. Delon always told me that he was going to marry me. I soaked his words up like a sponge. I had so much to learn about life. I was so naive when it came to relationships. When it came to Delon, I was gullible, but hey, I was young.

I was fifteen years old and in love with a roughneck. I had no idea what I was about to go through. I was going to learn just how hard life could be. In the beginning, things were pretty good with us. We enjoyed hanging out, dancing, and joking with each other. Several months into our relationship, things took a turn. After falling in love and discussing life, I found out that Delon had a baby boy. It broke my heart at first. I didn't know where I would fit in his life with a child in the picture. I was a child myself. I knew Delon loved me, but I didn't know how his obligation to his son would impact me. I wondered if he would get back with the mother and leave me. This was a girl he knew before me, and he had already gotten her pregnant before we met. However, he had not seen the baby because the girl's father kept him away. I told myself to be open and not let this be a monkey wrench in our relationship. He was so cute! He was in college, playing football. He could even dance well. This guy made me laugh, but he also made me cry. That's usually how relationships go, right? Up one minute down the next, then up again. We worked through the trials and hung in there longer than we should have. We overcame some challenges and made it through the first year together. At this point, I was sixteen, and Delon was eighteen. He was at the point where he wanted me to show him more of my love. Yeah, he tried to take us to the next level. I said no, but he ultimately forced himself on me, and the next thing I knew, I was in the emergency room because of him.

In retrospect, I wonder *why I did not scream my no to him? Why did I give in after saying no several times? Was I afraid?* I did not want to draw attention to what was happening; it wasn't rape. This was my boyfriend. *He would not do that to me*, I reasoned. I should have screamed, and I should have kicked him right between his legs. He would not have fought me back. I found out later that I could go toe-to-toe with him. My situation with Delon was not unlike what we see many young girls experience with boys who have not learned to discipline themselves concerning testosterone levels. As I think about it, Delon was disrespecting me. He was in his feelings and was not concerned about mine. Young women must demand respect. If the guy you have fallen for treats you like a piece of meat or property, nip it in the bud before it blooms into a nightmare of a relationship. It will get worse if you do not have boundaries and are not emphatic with your words. Concerning this situation, I was not ready. I had to come to terms with the fact that this guy I was so into actually took something from me. He took my body, my trust, and my mother's trust. *I had to tell my mom.*

"Mom, I told him I was not ready, but he kept pushing me to give in." I cried. "I can't believe he would force me into this. It is not right. Why would he do this to me?" I continued. "That bastard!" My mom yelled. She was so upset. "When I see him, I am going to give him a piece of my mind," my mom said in the angriest voice I ever had heard from her. "Mom, I have been calling him, but he's not answering," I said, disappointed. I even called his brother, and he had not seen Delon. This guy was ducking and dodging me on purpose. He knew he messed up. I was sixteen years old and laid up in a hospital bed, sick and in pain with an IV drip because of a bad sexual encounter with the guy who said he loved me, but forced me into sex. He really showed how much of a man he was not when he disappeared on me. This had my mom infuriated. She liked him; my brother liked him. He was so nice and charming. It was like allowing a wolf in sheep's clothing to come in and take advantage of your innocent little sheep. He was not going to get away with this by hiding out. I was intent on finding him.

I called all of the numbers I had for him; his mother, grandmother, brothers, and best friend. Finally, he called me. "Hello," I answer. "Hey, what's up?" He said in a low, almost shame-filled voice, better yet, a guilty voice. "I am recovering from PID, and you gave it to me. I told you no, and you forced yourself on me. Why, Delon?" I whined. "I don't know how you got that. If I gave it to you, I didn't know because I never had any symptoms," he defended himself. "Well, whether you knew or not, you were wrong to force me into that. I told you I was not ready. You were wrong, and I hate you for this." I hung up the phone in tears. I was embarrassed, humiliated, and feeling so ashamed. I felt like a fool for being in this situation. Thank God my mother was so understanding. She loved me through it, and so did my friends. A couple of days after my phone call with Delon, the doctor came in and told me that I was improving and I would be able to go home the next day. Concerned, I asked a question that had been on my mind. "Doctor, is this going to be with me forever?" He responded, "No, it is curable. The medication is doing its job and you will be fine." Needless to say, I was no longer thinking about having a boyfriend after that. I had stumbled over a rock, and that rock was Delon. I enjoyed my high school years, going to dances and hanging out with my girlfriends, but that whole boyfriend thing was not on my mind. I had my priorities straight: to graduate and go to college.

Well, that time came quickly. I was seventeen and in my senior year; wow! I will attend the prom, participate in all the senior year activities, and graduate. Wait a minute! Prom! I don't have a boyfriend. I do not have a date. Honestly, I didn't think I needed a date. I prefer going with friends. I asked my friend Mellie what her plans were. Mellie was tall, beautiful, and very smart. She and I had become friends over the two years I had started attending this high school. I was attending on a permit. My home school was not in the best neighborhood, so my mom transferred my little brother and me out of the district in the middle of our high school years. The friends I had at the previous school were the closest to me, but I made new ones pretty quickly. Mellie was one of the first few friends I made. She spent much of her time in the books, so I didn't think about the possibility of her already having a date when I asked her if she was going with anyone to the prom. She was going with Ricky. She was smiling when she let me know who her date would be. Then she asked me if I was going with anyone. I paused. I did not want to sound weird for not having a date. I gathered my nerves and gave my response.

"No, I don't have a date. I was thinking about going with just the girls, but you have a date, and I am sure Nicole has a date. Have you seen the way she and Donnie have been acting? They are so into each other. You cannot separate them."

"Yeah, they are an item," Mellie said.

"No worries, I will figure something out. I have to get to my art class. See you later!"

As I sketched my prom dress, my mind began to wander, *"Do I want a date? Do I really want to go with my girlfriends, or am I just putting up a block because there is no one special in my life right now? My dress is gorgeous. It looks like something made for a princess. I will go with this design.* I asked a lady at my church if she could make it. She was very good at making dresses. Ms. Kim said she'd love to do this for me. She got back to me about two weeks later for a fitting. When I put on the dress and looked at myself in the mirror, I felt beautiful. My mind was quickly transported to a page in a fairy tale book and I was a princess preparing for a coveted ball. Just as quickly as I transported, mentally, I returned to the space where I stood. I gave Ms. Kim a big thank you hug. I told her that I loved the dress. She thought I looked gorgeous in it and suggested I take lots of pictures. I let her know that I was definitely going to do that. I was so excited about getting all dressed up for this lifetime event. Senior year and the prom were all we heard about as we progressed through middle school and into our early high school years.

*** 

It's the big day! Makeup and hair; let's get it done! The glitz and glam of prom make a girl feel like a celebrity. We got our hair done in the most glamorous style we wanted. We had our choice of cars, within reason. Limo? Maybe. Classic Rolls Royce? Possibly. A sports car? That can happen. The pre-party was held at my cousin's beautiful house, and what a time we had as we took pictures and awaited the carriage. It was a popular Lincoln Towne Car at the time. The date situation was resolved. My brother's friend, Raffi, wanted to go with me since he did not have a girlfriend. Raffi was a nice guy. He loved to have fun, and his humor was great! We all hung out together anyway, so this worked out well for me. No ties. No pressure. We were just going as friends to have some fun.

We arrived at the Westin Bonaventure Hotel in Los Angeles in style. The hotel lobby was gorgeous. Gold posts and well-maintained entryways leading to the ballroom set the tone for a fantastic time in the spotlight. The guys were dressed in tuxedos or three-piece suits. Some of the young ladies wore hoop skirts under their beautifully draped satin gowns which poured over the undergarment, transforming them into princesses. Others wore fitted dresses displaying their "grown woman status." I stuck with the frilly Cinderella dress. I did not think about how I'd dance in the dress until I got to the dance floor. I would not be able to show off my skills since the dress covered my hips and legs completely. I did my thing, though. My girlfriends and I danced together even though they were there with their boyfriends. We danced to 1980s hip hop and R&B jams. Dancing with a guy with no obligation and no awkward feelings was great. This was the best prom date. I thanked Raffi for a fun time. There was no kissing. I had a good time.

Time rolled on and the big day was upon us. Caps and gowns are in effect. The bleachers were full of family and friends, waiting to cheer on their sons and daughters for a job well done. I was seventeen years old when I graduated. I did not make soma cum laude, but I graduated with honors! This may not seem like a big deal, but for me, I am happy to have made it out with a B average. I worked and went to school. It was not easy. I had formed a habit of completing my work at the eleventh hour. I wouldn't say I was a procrastinator. I have always juggled many different things, so I was not very good at leveling my load. I tried to do it all. No one could ever tell me I couldn't because I would not listen anyway. There was something inside of me that kept telling me I could do whatever I wanted to do. It did not tell me that I would be sacrificing health, time with family, and even friendships if I did not learn to pace myself.

My biological father attended my graduation. I was happy he shared this momentous time with me. I met my father later in life, a couple of years after my mom and adoptive father divorced. I was a pre-teen when my father first took my brother and me to hang out with him. He was not my brother's father, but he would take him whenever he picked me up. So many years had passed between my birth and the time we met that it was ironic when he introduced me to a distant cousin at my graduation. My dad's cousin had a daughter and stepson graduating from the same high school on the same day. I had an argument with her stepson on the city bus that transported us to school. He used to talk a lot of mess and I was tired of hearing it. One day I let him know he needed to chill out. It nearly turned into a fight. He was a popular guy, but I could care less. I have always believed everyone deserves the same respect, but my peers treated this guy like he was untouchable. His sister was popular, cute, and very nice. After two years of attending school with them, I found out we were related on graduation day. I am glad I didn't actually like the boy. That would have been something else. *Life is interesting.*

My next big life event after graduation was coming up; I was turning eighteen on June 21, 1986! Since I recently graduated, my mom decided to surprise me with a party at my aunt's beautiful, Victorian-style home in the heartbeat of Los Angles. I was surprised to see so many people. My biological father was there. It was funny because my aunt, who hosted the party, was married to my adoptive father's brother. The story behind that is an entire book by itself! I'll say this, my mom and dad had me at eighteen. My dad was not ready, and left my mom to handle it on her own. When I was just a few months old, my mom met a man who loved her enough to marry her and adopt me as his own daughter. He, unfortunately, was not at my party or my graduation, but he did show up a few months later when I needed him.

So back to the party. Quite a few people showed up to celebrate me, including my friends from my previous high school and the one I had just graduated from. Little did I know, a guy I met earlier in the year and had a crush on would be at my party. His sister and my mom were friends. He was a tall, good-looking brother of American Indian and Black descent. He was about three years older than me. I did not know much about his background, but he was cute. He was at my party with his sister. My aunt and female cousins seemed to think he was pretty cool. I danced with him most of the evening. We exchanged numbers, and I was on my way to falling for another guy because he looked good. I had no clue about what, if anything, he could bring to the table. I was eighteen and thought I was ready to handle the world. I was not. I had so much more to learn about men and life in general. I was still easily drawn in by superficial layers. I dated this guy, briefly and realized that he had nothing to offer me. I wish I had taken my time to get to know who he was before getting involved. I was not thinking. Google the word "dumb," and you will find that it is an informal word from North America defined as "stupid." Synonyms are unintelligent, ignorant, dense, mindless, and foolish. Young is described as an adjective and means having lived or existed for only a short time. When I reflect on my youth and young adult phase, I can apply these dictionary terms and see clearly that I was young and dumb when making decisions as a minor and as an eighteen-year-old.

## Reflection

*Is there any situation that you found yourself in and wondered how you got into that situation? Have you carried it with you throughout life? If you have not let it go, ask yourself what lesson you learned from it, then take the lesson, and leave the situation right where it happened. It's time to move in your resilience. You have a lot more life to live.*

# Chapter 2

# Street School

*The sidewalk curb that held the weight of my heavy heart became the platform from which I pivoted and started a new journey.*

MJEnvisionit

I was fresh out of high school, eighteen years old, and smelling myself, as grandma would say. Our grannies and aunties used this phrase to describe young girls who, in their minds, were moving too fast for their age or had a sassy mouth. I thought I knew it all, but I had no clue. The world was waiting to take me to another level of education... I went to street school. I was living with family and in college, but before I knew it, I was fighting with my uncle and had to move out. I did not feel it was right for him to tell me how to live, what time to come home, and put chores on me when I was an adult. I mean, dang! I was eighteen. Come on! My mother didn't even put chores on me. I did them on my own, not because it was an assigned task. On top of that, my uncle did not want me to have a boyfriend. He was very protective of his daughters, so he treated me the same way. I certainly was not feeling this whole situation.

I copped an attitude and left. I reached out to my best friend and asked if I could stay with her. Kyra is her name. Kyra and I went to middle and high school together until the end of tenth grade, when my mom transferred my brother and me into a different school district. I did not get to graduate with Kyra, but I was excited to attend college with her. She was intelligent, headstrong, and like me, she moved in with her family to attend school. Her family was a lot less strict than mine and always seemed to have a good time. I wanted that. I enjoyed the excitement. Her aunties and cousins would have weekend get-togethers playing table games, eating good food, and having alcoholic beverages available for anyone who wanted them. For an eighteen-year-old, this was precisely the kind of home I would prefer to stay in fresh out of high school. Freedom! No boundaries! Fun! Kyra and I would party and study. We'd stay up late but still got our assignments done. Thanks to a high-energy drink called Jolt. That was like a serious jet pack that could propel you from sitting with your head down and sleeping in the classroom to dancing on top of the desk. It was pure energy. Some might say crack in a bottle. Not appropriate for a Christian, but that was the language of that time of my life.

The year was 1986, and the drug epidemic was heightened. Hip-hop music was taking the world by storm, and I was no longer a little girl living at home with my mom. The days of walking with my brother home from school and supervising him while mom worked were over. I was grown and no longer living at home. I could make my own decisions and see whomever I wanted. Life Nikki's way was the best way, right? Wrong! We often hear that the grass is not always greener on the other side. Sometimes we get caught up in what we think we know but do not realize that we do not know much. That was especially true for me at eighteen years old. The situation that led to my night of drama and fall from grace, so to speak, did not have to happen. I resisted admonishment from my uncle, who simply cared about me. A man who knew what boys and men thought when they saw a girl that caught their attention. He was a man, for heaven's sake! I was a young girl, I had not lived long enough to determine if I were ready to be responsible for myself, but I pulled away from the covering my uncle provided. I made a dumb decision that resulted in my plummet to a sidewalk curb at two o'clock in the morning.

As I recall the dramatic event that changed my course, I realize that I have been telling myself it was not my fault that this older man was interested in me. It was not my fault that he took a liking to me while his wife lay up in a hospital bed giving birth to his child. Today, as an adult who has journeyed far beyond that period, I asked myself retrospectively, *was it my fault? Why didn't I tell Kyra about her cousin showing interest in me? If I were uncomfortable, why didn't I move out sooner?* As I contemplated what led to this huge blow-up between Mark and his wife, Angela, I realized that I should have seen it coming. I had blinders on, I guess. The man gave me a lot of attention. Anything I needed to do, he would offer to help me with it, or take me where I needed to go. I was not interested in him, but I was interested in how his mind worked. Mark was an entrepreneur. He was always looking for a business opportunity. He was not all that good-looking, but he was tall and athletic.

Mark and Angela had one toddler and another on the way. Angela was so sweet. She was soft-spoken and focused on her child. She cooked, washed clothes, and took care of the home. I think Angela was the kind of woman most men claim they are looking for, but she was not exciting. She was cute, but after taking on the role of wife and mother, Angela seemed to have forgotten what it took to lock in her husband. He needed attention from her. He needed her encouragement and support. Unfortunately, that was not top of mind for Angela, so he began falling for the young woman who seemed to give him what he thought he was missing. I can still hear it all playing in my head.

"Oh My God! What did you just say to her?" Yelled Angela.

"Huh? What are you talking about, Angela?" Mark responded as if he had no clue.

"Don't do that to me, Mark. I heard you. Really, you'd do that to me after I just gave birth to your child?" Pain poured from each word.

"Wait, baby, you are wrong. I haven't said anything." He continued in defense.

"You are lying! Get out! Get out! You are messing around with her!"

The scene at the house was too much. I ran out of the house, shaking in my pajamas, without shoes on my feet. I ran as far as I could and then just stopped. I was breathless. *"What just happened?"* I put my hands on top of my head and stood still in confusion. *How did we go from just watching TV, laughing at a scene, then all hell broke loose?* I walked over to the nearby curb and sat there with my head in my hands, trying to decide what to do next. I didn't know if I should call my mom, the new guy I was seeing, or my college buddy for help. It was a very cold and dark January night. At that moment, I could only think of getting off the streets. I did not know where to go. As I sat, tears streamed down my face. I asked God why this was happening to me? Why did I come out here to a city I didn't know, just to find myself sitting on the curb at two in the morning? I did not know what to do. I had exams coming up, my first semester was coming to an end, and I had no idea where I would live. The fight I had with my uncle was so bad, that I dared not call him to ask if I could return. I did not want to admit to him that I was wrong. I let pride get in the way, and for that, the trajectory of my life was a whirlwind. I had no idea where I would land. I was facing a situation that would not end as I had envisioned when I left for college. I was devastated sitting on that curb. The fight that this man had with his wife, over me was my official eviction notice. I was homeless.

I wondered to myself how this happened. My friend Kyra and I selected this great college in Northern California. She and I both had family near the college. It seemed the most reasonable choice. She moved in with her cousins and I moved in with my uncle. It was going well until I decided I was too grown to be subjected to my uncles' rules. I made a mistake by leaving, and now I had consequences to deal with. When we're young and inexperienced with life, we have no idea what evil lurks outside the security of our parents and family members who look out for us. Uncle Joe and Aunt Victoria were beautiful people who cared about their children and me. They were kind and excellent examples of what a Christian marriage should look like. Uncle, however, was just a little too strict for me. Not only was he too rigid for me, but he was also a bit too tough on his teenage daughter. This young lady was going through the boy-crazy phase. She wanted to have a boyfriend, but daddy would not allow it. She began sneaking out of the house, so she could do what she wanted without daddy's knowledge. I suggested that she sit her dad down to discuss her feelings, but she thought she could not talk to him. She planned on getting a job and moving out before graduating high school. Her goal was to be out of there by the age of seventeen.

My uncle was not the easiest person to talk to when it came to dating and just wanting to go out with friends. He was not trying to hear it. He cared so much for us that he pushed us away. He was so afraid of seeing us make wrong choices that he tried to shelter us from the realities of life. He didn't realize he was pushing his daughter into sneaking around, and me to the point of leaving. That is when I moved in with my friend Kyra and her family. I felt comfortable with them. They would visit Kyra in Los Angeles during the summer. I had not met everyone, but I had met Kyra's great aunt during one of her visits. At that time, she had come with one of her younger sons. I had not been introduced to the rest of the family until I arrived in the Bay area.

Kyra introduced me to her cousin Mark who was picking up his son and on his way to his car when we arrived at Kyra's great aunt's house. Immediately upon introduction, I could see that Mark was a nut! He liked to joke and have fun. Some of the stuff that came out of his mouth should have been recorded for a sit com. I later learned that Mark was very inventive. He was always thinking of a new invention to help him make millions of dollars. He was active with his son, too. His wife, Angela, on the other hand, was quiet. She did not have a whole lot to say. She thought his ideas were a little crazy. I am not saying that she did not support his ideas; I just do not recall her making very many supportive comments. Maybe it was because she was about eight and a half months pregnant with their second child. She was tired often. Angela was very attentive to their child. This could be why she never joined many of the business discussions. She was busy being a mom.

I thought Mark had pretty good ideas. I used to tell him that. I had and still have an entrepreneurial spirit. I am always supportive of anyone who can visualize themselves as a successful businessperson and take steps to make it happen. I am a natural encourager. I have come to realize this much later in life. Because of my desire to see others reach their goals, I get engaged in their conversations about new ideas, innovation, or business in general. This is both a good and bad thing for me. I think he mistook my supportiveness for something else. He enjoyed talking to me about his plans. He thought we would make a great team. He even told me he wished his wife had my ambition and drive. I did not think anything of it. I just told him that his wife was sweet and that she just had a different view of things. I did not know Mark was seriously thinking about being in a relationship with me.

A few weeks after I moved in, I needed to go shopping for a new car. My old car broke down, and my dad, the man who adopted me in my first few months of life, gave me money to buy a new one. I did not know the city, so I asked Mark if he'd mind taking me to shop for the car. He was happy to oblige. He took me to a few car lots. On the ride there, he talked to me about his business plans. I shared a few ideas with him. Toward the end of the conversation, he told me he was starting to feel something for me. He enjoyed being around me. I told him to step back and reminded him of his wife. I told him that we could never get together. He was married, and he was my friend's cousin. The whole thing would be wrong. I told him to just get that idea out of his head. I suggested that he try to make his marriage more exciting. He agreed and did not say anything more about it that day.

A couple of weeks later, Mark's wife went into labor. She was rushed to the hospital. Kyra and I stayed at the house and watched their little two-year-old. It was exciting. A new baby would be in the house. We were excited when Mark brought Angela and their new baby boy home. He was so cute and tiny. Kyra and I helped Angela with the little ones the first two nights she returned home. Angela was very weak. On the third night of Angela's return from the hospital, Kyra and her boyfriend decided to go out. I stayed behind to help Mark and Angela. Later that night, Angela had fallen asleep along with the kids. I had curled up on the floor in the front room to watch a little TV before going to sleep. Mark was on the couch in the front room, too. This is where we all hung out to watch TV. Mark wasn't ready to go to bed, so he stayed in the front room and watched TV with me.

Within thirty minutes, I dozed off. Mark, at some point, stretched his arm from the couch down to the floor and placed his hands under my blanket. He started rubbing my thighs. I awakened to his touch. I told him to stop. I told him he was wrong. He told me that he was falling for me. He wanted me. He wanted me to have oral sex with him. I told him no. Well, his wife heard part of the conversation. She was not asleep after all. "What did you say?" I heard her yell from the hallway. "What did you say?" Mark responded to Angela by playing the dumb role, "Angela, what's wrong? Why are you so upset?" Angela became louder, "I heard you." She was screaming and crying. Her heart was broken. It was an awful and sad scene. I panicked and left. I was never going to be able to stay in that house again. I could not take seeing the pain Angela was dealing with. I was also ashamed for not leaving the situation sooner. I was so scared. I guess I was afraid because I felt guilty. You see, I started developing feelings for Mark, too. I never told him, nor would I have. I would not have done anything to hurt Angela, but inside I was feeling something. I am glad this happened before that happened. If it had not, and I had continued dancing dangerously on the catwalk called temptation, I may have found myself in a forbidden relationship with a married man. This was my first semester in college, and I was already making a mess of my life. I was so young, so dumb.

I did not understand life yet. I could not believe what had just happened. I was sitting on a curb at two in the morning, not knowing what to do. I hugged my knees as tight as I could. It was cold, dark, and I was afraid. I prayed to God for forgiveness and help. I needed direction and a place to stay. I began to wipe my tears, took a deep breath, and came back to myself. I started looking around and realized that I was vulnerable in the dark. I got up and walked to the nearest phone booth. *In 1987, we were not using the small, compact cell phones available today.* Some people had the large and bulky car phone that looked like a box. I was not one of them. I had to find the nearest payphone.

I called my college friend, Trey. He was a frat boy, a member of Kappa Alpha Psi. We became friends when he invited me to a dance the Greek organization hosted when I first arrived at the campus. They knew how to throw a party, too. What I knew about guys in fraternities came from TV or movies. This was that they ran off of high testosterone and indulged in wild behavior. I did not see that with Trey. He was not like that at all. He was a gentleman, so I was comfortable reaching out to him. I went ahead and gave him a call, "Trey, can you come and pick me up? I am on the corner of S. Mathilda Ave and Cherrywood Dr. Something crazy has happened, and I need a place to stay for a while." Trey responded, "Sit tight. I am on my way."

Trey got to me pretty fast. He had a used 1982 Toyota Celica Supra. That was like having a used souped-up Honda Civic these days. Trey took good care of that car. He worked on campus, so he had a little pocket change to keep the car up and pay for his off-campus apartment.

"Ok, Nikki, this is it," Trey said as he walked me to his apartment door. He turned the key and escorted me in. "It is not much, but I have a place to sleep, shower, eat, and watch a little TV." "Yeah, way more than I have right now," I responded sadly. "It'll be okay. Go ahead and have a seat," Trey replied. "I'll make you some coffee or tea, pick one," he said. I sat down, "I'll just have some tea, thanks." I was still sobbing a bit. Trey brought the tea and sat down with me. I started explaining what had happened. I told him that I did not know what I was going to do. I had nowhere to go but back to LA. I wasn't sure if that was what I wanted to do, though. He told me to relax. He suggested I get a good night's sleep before making any decisions. Trey offered me his bed and said he would take the couch. I told him he did not have to do that. I would be fine on the couch; he just needed to bring me a blanket.

Trey walked over to the linen closet, reached in, and grabbed a sheet, a blanket, a washcloth, and a bath towel. He closed the door, turned and walked over to the couch, sat everything down, looked over at me and said, "Everything you need is right here. Finish your tea and then take a nice long shower. When you get out, I'll give you a massage to help relieve the tension in your body, if you would like". I thanked him again. I took my shower. It was relaxing. When I entered the living room area, Trey was in the kitchen. I thanked him for being there for me. He told me it was no problem. He asked me if I were ready for my massage. *I was.* He laid a blanket on the floor, helped me down, told me to lie on my stomach, and proceeded to rub me down with warm oil. He massaged my neck, my back, my hips, my legs, my ankles, and my feet. When he was done, he helped me up, put his T-shirt on me, then walked me over to the couch. He kissed me on my cheek and told me to have a good night's sleep. He told me he would be leaving for class at eight, but I could just lock the door behind me when I was ready to leave. I gave him a hug. Trey was a real gentleman. He did not try to have sex with me, at all. He did not take advantage of my vulnerable state. As I sat in his off-campus apartment, I realized that my future success in life, however I defined it, was dependent upon my mindset. If I settled in where I was at that moment: homeless, with no job, in a city far from my family, and feeling bad about myself, I may never achieve my goals. I had to figure out how to rectify the situation.

I called Kyra and asked her to get my things together and bring them to me. I also asked her to get in touch with my other friend, Frank. Frank was a guy I was fascinated with simply because he rode a NINJA motorcycle, drove a Chevy, and was on his way to the military. He was a young man who knew what he wanted and did not hesitate to go after it. He was different. He was not like the boys in the neighborhood I was used to. I met Frank through Kyra, too. We all hung out with one of her cousins at the local park. The park was very popular for car clubs, including low riders, to hang out. I met Frank there. The day we met was warm and sunny. Kyra and I drove to the park to see who was hanging out. The usuals were all there when we arrived. This included her cousin and his friend, Frank, who had taken to me quickly. He asked me if I wanted to ride on his motorcycle. I said sure. I hopped on the bike, wrapped my arms around his waist, and held on for dear life.

*"Whew! This wind is strong"*, I thought as the wind blew against my face. I buried my head into Frank's back to shield my face. We rode for about half an hour. When we returned, a few people had left, including Kyra. I did not know how to get back to her cousin's house so I could not give Frank directions. He invited me to stay with him for the night. I hesitated for a minute, but soon, I agreed. I was away in college. I did not have to answer to anyone, so I felt I was grown. I hopped back on Frank's motorcycle and rode with him back to his place. Frank lived with an older woman. She was a retired "lady of the night." She offered me dinner. I ate with Frank and the lady. She told us stories about her past escapades. It was pretty interesting. She had experienced all kinds of men. She could read a man all up and down. She could tell you precisely what kind of person a man was just by very few introductory words he speaks. I listened attentively and took mental notes. However, I have not applied the knowledge I'd gained from that conversation.

Thinking back on Trey and what a nice guy he was, I wonder why Trey and I never went out. Oh, I know what it was. Trey was one of the good ones; for some reason, I had a problem with falling for the good guys. It was almost as if I purposely repelled them so that they would not even try to step to me because I would do nothing but hurt their feelings. I seemed to attract the bad boys, those I could not hurt because they were too busy hurting me first. I was foolish to have not even considered Trey or a guy like him. What the hell was I thinking? I wasn't thinking at all. As a young girl, fresh out of high school, my relationship aptitude and my life navigational skills were nearly non-existent. I tried my best to change my ways. I always went for the roughneck or cute guy with "edge."

Frank did not have the rough exterior I was used to in a guy. He was soft-spoken, a hard worker, and on his way to the military. Frank was a guy with a plan for his life. He already knew he was going to the military; he already had plans to buy a home after and start his own business. He was different from the guys back home. Frank and I hit off pretty well in the first few weeks, so it was no wonder I reached out to him when all hell broke loose at Mark and Angela's. I could have stayed at Trey's, but I had been seeing Frank. Frank called me shortly after Kyra brought my things to Trey's house. He asked me what was going on. I told him it was a long story and did not want to go into details right then. "Frank," I said, "some crap happened at Kyra's cousin's house, and I do not have a place to stay. My friend from school will probably let me stay here, but I am not sure if I want to." Frank quickly replied, "You can come to my house. We have plenty of room. Don't worry about anything." I asked if he was sure. He said that he was very sure. So, I moved in with him and his roommate, a former lady of the night, Ms. Helen. Frank and I became a couple a whole lot faster than I would have ever imagined in times past. He took me to church with him. He introduced me to a family that was very close to him. He loved this family more than his own, it seemed. I must say, they were the sweetest people I have ever met. Frank seemed to surround himself with good people, even the ex-madame.

Frank went with me to purchase my new truck. The truck was a stick shift, and I did not know how to drive one of those. I wanted that truck badly. Frank promised to teach me how to drive it, so I bought the truck. Learning to drive a stick was scary, but I enjoyed it once I got it. I appreciated him supporting me while I tried to figure things out. Though Frank and I had become what seemed to be a perfect couple, I was not in love with him. I was still carrying feelings for someone else. I was still in love with a man back home in Los Angeles. This guy was tough, exciting, and popular. In contrast, Frank was a nice, educated military man. I was trying to break from the mold I was used to in LA when I met Frank. I kept telling myself that I needed to be with men who were doing something good with their lives. I needed to leave the thugs alone. I stayed with Frank for about four weeks before becoming homesick. I was ready to go back to Los Angeles. I missed home. I missed my family. I had been looking for jobs, but I did not have much luck. I needed a job to pay for my education. I was also getting tired of staying with Frank. I decided to go back to a L.A. I tried very hard to love him, but I never could. I cared for him. I was thankful for him but could not give my heart to him. This made things very difficult when I moved back to Los Angeles and found out some very surprising news.

### Reflection

*Have you ever stayed in a relationship with someone even though your heart was not in it? Did you do it for convenience, or were you just settling? At the end of the day, you hurt yourself or the other person if you are not honest about your feelings.*

# Chapter 3

# He Left Us, but God Kept us

*It is an empowering feeling when you can lean on a power greater than your own to lift you out of the muck when the person who should have been there was not.*

**MJEnvisionit**

"**M**om, I am coming home," I declared. "Baby, what is going on?" Mom said. Mom, I have gone through so much, and I want to tell you about it, but right now, I just can't. I cannot stay here any longer. When I return to L.A., I will find a school out there." Mom was sweet. She told me to come on home. I told Frank my decision, and he wasn't too happy about me leaving. It was February 1987, and Valentine's Day was approaching. Frank wanted me to stay, but I told him it was not a good idea because I missed home. I needed to be around my family. Life was just going wrong, and I needed to start over. Frank later understood. Since I wanted to take my new truck with me, and it was a stick, Frank offered to drive me back home, and he would fly back. He was so supportive of my decision and good to me. The drive back to L.A. was uneventful. We listened to good music. He and I talked about life and his upcoming deployment. He had enlisted in the Navy and would be shipping out soon.

"Mom, this is Frank. He has been a very good friend to me and has helped me through the mess I was going through up north." Mom, being the nice person she is, gave Frank a big hug and asked him to stay for dinner. He could only stay a little while since he had to catch the plane back home. Frank enjoyed meeting my mom. She had a lot to say. My mom can talk to anyone about anything; she never meets a stranger. Frank shared a little about his parents and how their divorce impacted him. He was close to both parents, but you could tell he resented that they were no longer together. He blamed his father's second wife for their break up. My mom encouraged him to let go of those feelings and focus on the good. The conversation turned to me. They both talked about how headstrong I was. Frank couldn't resist talking about how I really wanted the pickup truck, but it was a stick shift. I did not know how to drive a stick, however. I wanted it so bad, that I got it anyway. Frank told how he had to drive it off the lot and helped me drive it from Northern California to Southern California. Since Frank was enlisted in the military, he was scheduled to start basic training and to ship out on an assignment. "Frank, I appreciate all that you have done. I will miss you." *Oh, but little did I know that I would not be breaking up with him for long.*

Two weeks after Frank flew back to Northern California, I began going through changes. I was tired often, and I was late starting my period. I figured I was just going through a phase of irregularity. As a little more time passed, I began to get sick in the mornings. I was not eating much but vomiting up a syrupy orange fluid. My mom was starting to wonder what was going on. Honestly, I think she had mother's intuition about something I was unaware. She suggested I see a doctor. I arrived at the clinic. This was a free health center in my neighborhood that many of the girls I knew went when they thought they might be pregnant, or had been given an infectious disease after a bad sexual experience. I was hoping I did not see anyone I knew as I sat waiting to for the doctor to let me know the results. I braced myself when the nurse called my name.

Moments later, I was in my head space asking, *are you kidding! What! No, I can't be pregnant! I am not ready to have a child. I still have school to finish. I would be a single mom. That is not part of my plan.* I had to have a heart to heart with my mother.

"Uh, Mom, are you in the middle of something?" My voice caught in my throat, nearing a whisper.

"No, I am not. What's up, Hun?" she responded in her usual loving voice.

"I don't want you to be upset with me, but I just found out that I am six weeks pregnant." I couldn't believe the reality of it as I stood before my mother.

"Oh, baby," her tone turned sorrowful, "what are you going to do?"

Without hesitation, I quickly replied, "well, I am still going to finish school. I will not let this stop me. I know you were a single mom for a long time and did a good job, so I know I can do this. I will push and make a good life for my child and me." I was determined beyond measure. Perhaps too determined. Mom's next question was, had I told Frank yet? I didn't tell Frank first because this was something I was more comfortable sharing with my mother first. I would tell him next.

Later that night, I called Frank. I told him the news. He was excited. Neither of us committed to getting back together, but we were excited about the baby. We talked about our future as parents and individually. Frank already knew what he wanted to do once he completed military service. He wanted his own business. Frank was in the Navy and had received orders for Desert Storm. He was about to ship out soon. He told me he would call or write to me once he reached his destination. He also committed to sending me money to make sure I had what I needed for the baby. After our last call, I had not talked to him for almost a month.

It has been over a month since he and I spoke. He said he would call once he got stationed or at least write to me. I have heard nothing."

It seemed like forever since I last spoke to Frank. I was worried. I called his sister, and she told me that he was likely still out to sea. So, I got smart. My investigative senses kicked in, and I figured out how to locate him. I called World Locaters. I gave them the information I had, and soon enough, I was given a phone number to call in Washington D.C. that would lead me to Frank. I called the number and left a message with Frank's commanding officer for him to get in touch with me as soon as he touched land. I got my call. God is amazing!

"Hello, yes, this is Nikki. Who am I speaking to?"

"This is Chaplain Murray. I have Frank with me...just a moment." I heard the phone being passed.

"Hi, Frank."

"Hi, Nikki."

I started in with my burning question for him, "So, what took you so long to call me?" *He probably could feel the heat off of my skin through the phone.*

"I spent all that time on the sea. I could not call. As soon as I got off the ship, I got the message, and I am calling now." Frank was apparently irritated by my question.

"Ok, are you still going to send money to help me out?" I asked him this with a serious attitude. I was not ready for his response, either.

"Uh, let's talk about that. I have been talking to some of the guys on the ship, and I realize I am not ready for this. I want to live my life, and I am not ready for the responsibility."

I wanted to reach through the phone, and I put my hands on him. "What! I am nearly four months pregnant. Why are you telling me this now? I want to live my life, too. I am not ready, but I am also not afraid of handling my responsibility. You and I laid up like grown folks and made this baby, so you and I are responsible for it." Frank had his mind made up and decided he was not going through with it. He coldly told me that he was sending money for an abortion. I explained to him that I was not going to do that. I was taking responsibility for my action. I was not doing it alone, either. Oh yes, I kept the number to World Locaters. So, while Frank traveled the seas and did his part to protect our Nation, I was back in the U.S., giving birth to his son.

Once I had my beautiful baby boy, I located Frank. The Chaplain took my information, called me back once he had Frank in the office, and told me that the military takes the responsibility of children seriously. Their policy would not allow a man to be in the military and not take care of his child. He put Frank on the phone and let Frank tell me that he was acknowledging the baby as his dependent and was setting up financial allotments for his care. This took some of the financial load off of me. I thought as long as I had financial help from him, I could do the rest. Why not? Most of the women I grew up around were either single moms or strong women who were the backbones of their families, with a husband or without. So, I could do it too.

After the call and a few minutes spent pondering the idea of single parenting, my mom and I heard a knock at the door. Mom yelled from the kitchen for me to get the door since she was cooking. I walked over to the door in shorts and a t-shirt. To my surprise, Mr. Roughneck was at the door. I had not seen him in quite a while, but I reached out to his mom during the first two months after I got to college. She told me he was in jail. I wrote him once or twice. He wrote back, saying he was still into me and proud of me. I had mixed emotions about seeing him.

"So, when did you get out?" I asked

"Yesterday," he said while looking me up and down. We chatted a bit; then I told him I was pregnant. He was hurt. He did not expect to hear that from me.

"Wait! What are you tripping off of, Delon?" I asked with an attitude.

I wasn't sure how to respond when he said, "I have always seen you as this beautiful, strong woman who was going to get all kinds of degree, and probably become mayor of the city." Delon chuckled as he ended his "all hail the queen" accolades. I explained that being pregnant would not stop me from achieving my goals. My mother did it. She raised my brother and me without our father's help. She went to school after work a couple of days a week. I know I can do this. I will never stop pursuing my education. I was adamant!

The next question I had to tolerate was one I had been expecting to hear. Delon asked if I was still with the father. I told him yes, because I was, at least at that moment. Delon told me he was still in love with me, and if it did not work out with my baby's father, he would be his father. He always wanted to marry me. My pregnancy did not stop Delon. He just hung around in the background. I tried very hard to act like I did not want to be bothered with him anymore. My poker face was weak. Delon knew I still cared, even though my mouth said something different.

"Well, Delon," I said calmly, "I need to get back to what I was doing, so you will have to leave. It was nice to see you."

"It's always nice to see you. Congratulations, I hope he makes you happy,"

Delon just had to add that little statement, but I know he was hoping the man I was pregnant for would not make me happy. Delon wanted me with him. I felt so many emotions after I closed the door and watched Delon walk away from my living room window. I felt sad because Delon and I always said we'd be married and have kids together. I was not all in with my baby's father because, honestly, I was not planning on getting pregnant. I had not known Frank very long. I had just completed my first semester of college, and Frank was in his first few months with the US Navy. I was going to be a first-time mother, and I was going to do it alone.

If I had allowed my mind to stay on that curb too long, sulking in sadness, I would have become stuck in the place of impact. The sidewalk curb that held the weight of my heavy heart became the platform from which I pivoted and started a new journey. I could have wallowed in the mess I made out of my life. I did not, thank God. Unfortunately, not everyone knows how to pull themselves out of sinking sand. When trauma hits, it leaves an impact. It is up to us to decide how long we let it hold us down. The good thing to know is that we have the power to move from that place by taking control of our mindset. Defeat, or victory for me was based on how I viewed it. I decided I wanted to be victorious. I chose to push forward. This is not easy for everyone. Your mind has to be in a state that is strong enough not to allow thoughts of defeat or worry to take a seat and just hang out. Your mind has to be aware of tactics that the enemy of our destiny uses to break us down and keep us from achieving what we desire in life.

I desired to complete college and had no plans of becoming a mother at eighteen. I was not sure how to feel about it at first. I was concerned with what my mom, dad, grandpa, and others would think about me. In preparation for any negative comments, I started working out in my head that I would provide for my kid with or without a man. I was going to buy diapers, clothes, and food. *I got this*, became my motto, and, later, the armor that kept good men away from me. I took control of my narrative by anticipating the negative-Nancy comments and having a response ready for it. My experience in life has shown me that our mindset is everything! We can think positively long enough to bring ourselves into a state of bliss. We can think negatively long enough and sabotage every blessing that was stored up for us. I chose to think positively about my ability to handle parenthood and school. It is essential to keep the mind filled with thoughts that can drive you forward, not keep you stuck in disappointment or resentment.

As a young woman, I realized that we have the ability to overcome anything that tries to stop or resist us. We overcome the resistance through what we believe and speak. If we think and believe we are failures and we confess it out of our mouths, then failure is what we become. On the other hand, if we believe and say that we are victorious, then we shall become winners. I believe there is a war going on in the world of thought. Joyce Meyers describes it as the "battlefield of the mind." Her book, Battlefield of the Mind, addresses mindset. She talks about how worry, doubt, confusion, anger, depression, and so much more can be controlled by us.[3] We can change our thinking. She does this from a biblical perspective. I have always believed it was up to the individual to take control of his or her thoughts. I figured it out from reading the Bible. Many scriptures speak against worry and fear. For example, Matthew 6:34 KJV says, "Take no thought for tomorrow, for tomorrow will take care of itself." I have realized that we have the choice of living in heaven on earth or hell on earth. That choice is heavily influenced by the way you think.

In studying the Bible, we learn that words shaped the world. The Gospel of John identifies the Word of God as Jesus, the Messiah. Logos is the Word of God, or principle of divine reason and creative order (Dictionary.com). If words shaped the world, what were the thoughts behind those words before they were spoken? The mind of God cannot be explained, yet His intention can be derived from the fruits of the words He spoke. The God-thought manifested in words. God's words manifested the creation. In the book of Genesis 1:26 KJV, "God said let us make man in our image, after our likeness." If the Bible is true, and I believe it is, doesn't this mean that we, as the creation of God who has been formed in His image, have the power to speak life to the words? God speaks to His creation and establishes order. It is when we are out of order that bad situations seem ten times worse than they are. When our health is bad, or our emotions are at a level ten on an ascending scale of one to ten, anxiety arises, putting you in a state of worry. If you do not recognize and correct it immediately, you will find yourself in a cycle of ongoing defeat. The defeat is then caused by your uncontrolled thoughts that must be bought into order. When we allow negative ideas about a situation to permeate our lives, we can find ourselves imprisoned in a never-ending story of the victim. This mindset can keep you shackled, thus holding you back from becoming who God purposed you to be!

### Reflection

*Have you ever stayed in a relationship with someone even though your heart was not in it? Did you do it for convenience, or were you just settling? At the end of the day, you hurt yourself, or the other person, if you are not honest about your feelings.*

# Chapter 4

# Single and losing it: I don't want to be Superwoman!

*Superwoman? Is that a compliment? Go ahead; get caught up trying to live to that title. You can wear the Super Woman cape, but be careful before you find yourself flying high on a false sense of security in yourself. Watch out when reality sets in, and you find yourself falling quickly into an abyss of loneliness and pain.*

**MJEnvisionit**

*Superwoman!* That is what some people called me. "You are awesome girl! I don't know how you do it. You know, raising a child, working full time, and going to school." I would tell them it was only with God's help. Then I'd ask myself, *"Am I really superwoman or is it all a façade? Am I doing the right thing in going hard for my purpose, or am I hurting my child?"* I remember so clearly how I spoke to my precious little guy. It was not always in a loving manner. If I felt rushed for work or had to get a paper finished for school, I would get frazzled and impatient. I had no idea what I was doing to my son's psyche by projecting my pressure-filled life on him. I was so young. I was around twenty-one when Tyrell began pre-school. Having him there helped me since I was trying to complete my education and work. I was motivated and wanted so much out of life, but having a baby at that time was not in the plan. I mishandled the most precious time of my son's life by not focusing on his emotional development and security needs as a pre-school-aged little boy. I put more attention on my education and career than on him. I still picture the mornings when I would fuss and complain because my little boy was not moving fast enough for me.

"Get up, hurry up and get dressed. I am late. I have to be at work in thirty minutes. Hurry Up!" I'd say like a commander instead of a mommy. He'd reply in the sweetest little voice telling me, *Mommy, I'm sleepy.* I would act as if I didn't care. I remember telling him that I had to go to work. That I couldn't be late anymore and to come on. *Really?* Like a three-year-old knew what that meant. I was reacting out of frustration, which grew as I watched time slipping away. It was getting later; I reached out and grabbed my son with both of my hands, my right hand gripping his left arm, and my left hand gripping his right arm. My aggressive hold scared him. Tears rolled down his face and it shook me. "Oh baby, I'm sorry. I did not mean to make you cry. Please stop crying. I have to get you to school so I can get to work." I wanted to cry with him. I was upset with myself for reacting the way that I did. I never wanted to hurt his feelings or make him afraid. My mom would always save the day but would be highly upset with me.

That day, Mom came into my room with an attitude toward me. She was not having it. She took over and told me to go on to work, and she'll take her grandson to pre-school. I responded asking how she would be able to do that if she had to go to work too. I loved her reply, she said, "I do, but I can let them know I will be late, you go on. I am tired of you yelling at that baby." That hit me. It is nothing I am proud of. I wish it never happened, but it is my reality and his. I don't know why I was so afraid to tell my job I was running late. I think I was not sure if I would get fired or warnings, but I just couldn't let myself be late. You'd wonder why I couldn't just get up earlier. The problem was that I took on too many things. I was always trying to prove that I could do it all. Well, the truth was… I could not. Something had to take a back seat; it was my child and later my health.

I wonder how many young mothers or fathers can relate? How often have our children paid the price for our unwise decision-making? How often do we unintentionally neglect the needs of our children? Neglect is a strong accusation. I could have easily argued that I provided a home, food, clothing, love, activities, and everything my child needed, so there was no neglect. I was not running after men or hanging out in the streets often. I was not beating my child. What I did, however, had the same impact as if I had been doing those things. I spent too much time making up for not having a father in the home to help me with my son. I worked a lot. I got my education and I was able to put my son in a Christian school. I was proud of these accomplishments. I felt like I was doing the right thing for him. Unfortunately, he did not reap the benefits for long. Instead, my baby was lacking supervision and leadership from a strong male figure. His father was in his life on a part-time basis. This made it hard on me and in turn, hard on my son. Out of my stress, I yelled as if this innocent little boy was making me late on purpose. As if he understood that if I were to arrive late too many times, I may not have a job, or, I would not get to the next level. That was a "me" problem, not his. He just wanted my and his father's attention.

Sometimes children become the unsuspecting victim of situations their parents find themselves in. Besides examples where parents outright blame their kids, or physically abuse them, some impacts are subtle. It may be the words you say in the presence of your child about your own life, or said feelings about the absent parent that can leave an emotional scar on the child. You may have occupied yourself with so many things that you never allow time to play and laugh with your child as often as he or she needs you to. My son was crying out for attention, and I did not realize it until it was too late. Why? I did not think he was lacking it. I did so much for him. He was always well-dressed. I took him to children's church. He had wonderful godparents and an awesome grandmother. His father was not estranged from his life, but he lived seven hours away. He would send for him and I'd put him on a plane to go and spend the holidays and summer with his father.

My focus was on how to go another level, up. I did not want to stay at one level. I needed, wanted to make more money. I wanted to be a homeowner; I had no desire to stay in an apartment for the rest of my life. I wanted more, but my desire for more caused collateral damage. Entering the world of motherhood shortly after graduating from high school, and only six months after beginning my higher education journey, was, to say the least, disappointing and challenging. I was stressed out, but did not know it. I became a workaholic, burying myself in work, education, and creating more work. I was so determined to make it. I wanted to prove to myself and anyone watching me that I could do it all. I can be a single mother, work, attend school, and raise my little boy. It was true; I could do it all. I did not realize that doing it all did not include quality. The quality of life I wanted for myself was ironically pushing my son off in the distance. I focused so much on making a living and obtaining my college degree that my precious child was fading into the fabric of life and circumstance.

A typical morning for this so-called superwoman was Rush, Rush, Rush. So much pressure, pressure on herself, and more importantly, pressure on her young preschooler. What kind of impact did that lifestyle have on this child? How did he handle it? I recall one of those mornings when I was rushing to get us dressed and out the door for work and pre-school. I can still see his face, tears in his eyes, and sniffling while saying, "Mommy, I'm dressed." Nana came in to help him. She did not want to hear me yelling at him another day. Nana always saved the day. Nana was concerned about her grandchild and me. She would make me get off the phone if she thought that baby was being ignored. She knew what it took to be a real mother and still does. Back then, I had a lot to learn. I was stressed, but I did not see it for myself. I see it in retrospect. I had this mentality that I could do it all. Nothing was going to hold me back. I was trying to prove to myself and others that having a baby out of wedlock and so young would not stop me. I refused to be another unwed, young mother on welfare. My push to be better than I was brought frustration into our lives.

Sometimes, I would snap at my precious little blessing as if he were the cause of my frustration. I would get upset if he did not move fast enough. I was not handling it well at all. At the time, I had not recognized my blessing as such. I kept stumbling over him, thinking he was getting in my way, not to stop me from having fun or anything like that, but slowing me down from achieving the "American

Dream." I wanted my degree, my own home, and nice things. The only way I believed I could get it was by going for it with all my energy and doing so with blinders. I can only imagine what was going through his mind when he heard his mommy yelling and being so angry. He had no idea how to process all of this. I wondered if he realized that mommy loved him, but mommy was just having a bad day. It is crazy how you can reason later on, but when you are in an emotionally taxing situation, your mind can take you to a place of defense: defense of a position or defense of action.

We say things like, "*well, if this had not happened, then I would not have done that.*" To defend our position, we may declare, "no one is going to do it for me, so I depend on myself." It is a way of deflecting from ourselves. We can behave irrationally when our anxiety level is high, and our adrenaline is racing. We regret it later, but the action has taken place, or the words have left your mouth, and you cannot take it back. Pride had me thinking I was Superwoman and could do it all. *Superwoman? Is that a compliment or a curse?* Go ahead; get caught up trying to live to that title. You can wear the Superwoman cape, but be careful before you find yourself flying high on a false sense of security in yourself. Watch out when reality sets in and you find yourself falling quickly into an abyss of loneliness and pain. I don't know about anyone else, but unless God is leading and directing, your Superwoman title has no power.

Let me tell you what I mean. Today, you decide, "I got this." Even if you claim to be a believer in God the Father and quote scriptures such as, "I can do all things through Christ who strengthens me," recognize that you can do these things; however, there is also a cost of doing too much. There is a cost of taking the attitude that you do not need anyone but you and God. Don't get me wrong. We all need God; however, if you are not mindful, you can shut out the very help God has placed in your life. It is okay to say I need a little help from a human being. It is okay to say I made bad choices, but I am ok, and I am growing and learning from those things. You do not have to be so tough that you hide all the pain in your heart because you are disappointed in yourself for those choices.

I believe that when you refuse to acknowledge the downside of bad decisions and you choose to suppress them by becoming a high achiever, or a workaholic, you never deal with the hurt at its root. You end up building a brick wall that guards your heart, and no one can get in, not even the person God might be sending to be a blessing. Go on, Superwoman! Do your thing and keep that roughneck in your life. He brings excitement to you. Never mind that this man does not have a stable job. You don't care because *you got this*. You don't need that blessing God left at the brick wall just for you.

## Reflection

*Have you inadvertently shut out the people who matter more when you've focused too much attention on the things you thought mattered most?*

# Chapter 5

# Life With a Drug Addict

*In our youth, we look toward adulthood as if it were an Olympic medal, only to be met with surprise that, instead of getting the gold, the silver, or the bronze, our prize is that we made it through that race and are prepared for the next.*

MJEnvision1t

Dating again! I went back to my first love. Little did I know he was addicted to drugs.

I went backward. What the Hell was I thinking; *drugs, women, lying, and stealing*? My life was crazy with him. A few months after re-enrolling in college, I started talking to Delon again. At first, it was just on a friendship basis. Later we started digging each other again. Yes, even after all the drama. Even after I had a child with someone else, he wanted me, and I realized I liked him. Plus, I could use his help with my son while I went to work and school. It was more beneficial to me that he was not working a consistent job. He could help me get through school, and since I made ok money, I could take care of the bills. I could be Superwoman with him. Delon came to me with a request I did not want to refuse.

"Hey, Nikki, my grandmother owns some apartments on Crenshaw. What do you think about moving in there together? He asked. "Yeah, that would be cool. Let's do it", I responded excitedly. Two weeks later, we were moving into the apartment. I was happy to be back with my first love, even after all of the hell he put me through. I was a go-getter, so having a boyfriend who was the opposite of me, worked in my favor. He was not working. The deal was that he would watch my little boy while I went to school and worked. I didn't mind, initially, because I needed this kind of help. He loved him like his own son, so why not let him be the stay-at-home dad? This is the same guy that was hurt when he found out I was pregnant with my son. He told me he'd step in and be a father to my son if his father and I didn't work out. For about a month, this was working out ok. It was just reversed roles. I'd get up and head out to work without the time constraint of having to drop my son off at daycare. I was happy to let my little guy sleep in because I hated the morning struggle we went through to get up and out the door on time. This was good until I started noticing things.

I came home from work one day. Delon was sitting in the dark. The TV was missing. "Where is the TV?" I asked, puzzled. Delon responded nervously, "Baby, I had to sell the TV." I couldn't imagine why he would do such a thing. "Why?" I asked. "I needed to pay a bill, and I didn't have any other option," he said almost convincingly. I was upset because that was his grandmother's TV. I told him he needed to get it back. He said he couldn't. I left it alone. The following week, I came home from work and saw that my bike was missing. I asked what happened to the bike, and Delon explained that he owed money to someone. I was furious and yelled, "For what? Are you doing drugs?" Delon replied so pitifully, "Yeah, baby, but I am going to stop. I feel bad. I keep hurting you. I can't be doing this." I was beyond angry. I screamed, "Damn it, Delon. What the hell were you thinking? My bike? Really? You need help! I am scared of what you will do next. You are not keeping my son anymore. I don't want you to end up putting him in danger. Oh, and I am moving back with my mom." After all the yelling, I told him to take me to my bike. I was going to get it back. I am so glad my son was with my sister-friend on this day.

Delon and I got into my car and drove a few miles until we arrived at what I have termed a "zero-star" motel on Century Boulevard in Inglewood, CA. I gave the name Zero-star because it was the bottom of the bottom. This particular area was known for heavy prostitution and drugs. The motel was where street transactions took place; you can call it street commerce of the illegal kind. I was not in my sound mind at the time. I was upset and couldn't think clearly. I pulled up right in front of the motel door where the drug dealer and my bike were located. I told the guy I was there for my bike. He told me I had to pay to get it back. I told him the bike was stolen from me and I'd just have the police get it. I even had the nerve to say to the drug dealer that I am not the one using drugs, so I do not have to pay for it. I ended with, "just give me my bike." You know what? I got my bike back. Nothing but the Blood of Jesus that covered me in this situation. I knew very early that God protected me. I have believed in God since I was a little girl, but as a teenager, I learned about salvation and gave my life to Christ. It did not keep me from sinning or making mistakes, but it kept me protected. It also kept me from staying in low places. I would feel guilty or convicted whenever I messed up, but I would repent and try to do better. I had a sense of boldness because of my faith. I am sure that is why I had no fear in standing up to that drug dealer and the one after that. You see, Delon had a long way to go. I was not in a good situation with him. I needed to get out. I was tired. I told him I was leaving.

I remember hearing Delon plead, "Baby, don't leave. I love you. I am going to change. I don't want to be like this. I need you to help me through this." My heart sank. I don't know if it was because I loved him or if it was my overly empathetic character trait, but I gave in to him. No, I did not stay in the apartment. I went home to my mother, but I still saw Delon. My mom stepped in and helped me with my son, too. After the incident with him four years ago, she forgave Delon. Delon was charming. He could melt your heart with his looks and boyish way of talking himself out of trouble. It was as if he was just a naïve little boy who meant no harm, but did stupid things. I had to forgive and give him another chance. Little did I know it would be one more chance, then another.

Shortly after I moved back with my mom, she got Delon a job where she worked. He was doing pretty good for the first month. He learned the job pretty well. He was stocking the warehouse and picking orders. One of the company's owners was impressed with him, so he asked Delon to take on a new task. Delon had to get parts from one location and deliver them to another. One day, on payday, he had the task of picking up payroll checks and taking them to one of the company locations. Delon disappeared. He never returned to our work site. We waited and waited. I called everywhere looking for him. I did not know if something had happened to him, or if he slipped back into his habit. He finally showed up a few hours later than he was supposed to. The company truck was a little scratched and a big tree branch was in the back of the truck. He said he had an accident. It looked like and smelled like a lie. The big question was coming, that is, where's the payroll bag? It was there and intact. Thank God. He did not steal the money. But what really happened? Did he get high? Who knows? It was payday, after all. Delon got fired after that situation. He could not be trusted. It all seemed too suspicious. The company did not want to risk anything while doing a favor for my mom on behalf of me.

I hated him, but I loved him. I would contemplate whether to give up totally on him, or keep trying to help. I was trying to figure out how to get him to see himself the way I saw him. I shared my faith in God with him and I would tell him he needed to trust God to bring him through the addiction. I wanted him to get help more than he did. I really did not know how to handle him. Was I to stand with him, be supportive, or leave him so he could learn on his own? Those are a few of the many thoughts that ran through my mind. It was too much, but I have always been one to take on more than I should. I was in college, still chasing that degree, and working. I could not focus on school or my job when Delon would not return my call. He would go missing one or two days, then return as if nothing happened. Something always happened. I would be afraid that when I got off work, I'd find out that something had gone wrong with Delon. Worry and anxiety consumed me. I'd ponder, *"Where is he? Why hasn't he called? Is he dead, or in jail?"* I needed to know where he was so, I'd leave work early to go find him. This was getting out of control. I would find him at his grandmothers or at his aunt's house. I'd yell, fuss, and fight, then I'd be all hugged up with him again.

I remember one Friday night I wanted to go hang out with Delon. I called his grandmother and asked to speak to him. She'd let me know he wasn't home, but he may be at his aunt's. I would thank her and ask her to have him call me when he returned. Next, I would call his aunt. I would get the same reply; Delon was not there. I had become more and more worried, so I would pray for his protection and wait to hear from him. A couple of days later, the phone would ring and Delon would be the voice on the other end. He behaved as if nothing was wrong.

"What's up? Can I come see you?" This is how he started the conversation.

"No, no you can't. I am tired of this. You are doing these disappearing acts on me like you did when you were on drugs. You take off on Friday and I hear from you on Sunday night. Are you back using drugs?" I let my anger drop down a few levels as I was relieved to hear him say he was not doing drugs. I continued inquiring about his whereabouts. "So where were you?"

"I went out to Riverside with my dad," Delon's words poured out of his mouth easily.

"Oh, ok. You could have called to let me know that. I don't want to be worrying about you". I knew he was lying, but I chose to believe him. I was hooked.

"So, can I come see you," he asked.

"Yeah, come on," I gave in easily.

Delon came over and we hung out for a little while. I told him that the following Saturday I had to take a test at Los Angeles Community College and I needed him to watch my son. He suggested that he ride with me and keep my car. He would take my son with him to his grandmother's until I was done testing. I agreed. The days that followed were uneventful. We talked on the phone. Laughed and joked about what we saw on television, or teased each other about who could dance better. Saturday arrived quickly. It was time for me to head over to the college to take my exam. This was for a job with the County of LA. Delon rode with me and then took my car and my son to his grandmother's house.

A few hours later the test was over. Delon knew what time he was supposed to come back, but he was not waiting outside when I was done. I went to the phone booth and called his grandmother to see if he was at her house. She thought he might be in the back room, but he did not answer when she called him. I asked to speak to his dad, who was living there. He answered, and I told him I was stranded and needed a ride back. He told me Delon he would come and get me. I asked him where my son was and he said he was with him. He was bringing him when he comes to pick me up. When I got in the car, I asked if Delon was using again. He said he didn't know. When I got to the house, I was pissed off. I went into the house and to the back room where he stayed. He was asleep. I shook him and cursed him out; then I pounded him with my fists. He woke up and said he was just tired. I did not really buy it, but I loved him so much that I gave him another chance. He could never drive my car again, but I was still hanging in there with him.

Eventually, Delon found another job, but that did not last long. He was there a couple of months before he started missing work. One day, I called his job and the manager told me he did not come in. I made a beeline to his aunt's apartment; he had moved out of his grandmother's house and in with his aunt so he could go to work in her area on the west side of L.A. I arrived at his aunt's and knocked on the door. Delon did not answer. I banged on the door; someone opened it. I had no idea who this was.

"Hi, I am here for Delon," I said.

"Come in," the strange guy offered.

I looked around his aunt's place. I was trying to figure out what he was doing with these strange people. "Why is that girl blow-drying her hair in your aunt's bathroom, Delon? Are you screwing her?" I asked, miffed. As soon as I asked that question, another girl came out of his aunt's bedroom. "Delon, what is going on and who are these people? Are you doing drugs in here? He didn't have any answers. He just stood there looking stupid and I felt stupid. As I started yelling at those people to leave, I heard a knock at the door. I went to answer, but Delon beat me to it. To my surprise, there stood Mr. Drug Dealer. The plot thickens. As the saying goes, real life is stranger than fiction. This man was coming for his money.

"Where's my money?" he asked.

"What money," I snapped back, although he was talking to Delon.

"This 'nigga' owes me for my dope." He said emphatically.

"Well, write it off as a loss and maybe the Lord will have mercy and forgive you for the lives you are destroying. Take this as an opportunity to get your life right. Please leave." I pleaded. He just looked at me. I continued, "Ask God to open your heart and forgive you if you walk away from this one." God must have been with me. That drug dealer left and so did all those people without any extra drama. In all of this, you may be wondering where was my son?

As I write, I have to think for a moment. *Was I focused on my son or this man? Did I spend as much time caring for the baby boy I brought into this world as I did trying to help Delon? What was I thinking?* As hard as I tried to improve myself through continuing college and working a decent job, I missed what was right in front of me. I had a son who was watching how I interacted with this drug-addicted man. I was fighting, crying, and not spending quality time with my child. I was essentially a mother to a grown man and a little boy. My mind was on the wrong thing. I know a few women who have been there and a few who are there now. I share the wisdom I have gained so they will hopefully stop and think about the consequences their children will suffer if they keep focusing on everything but the child or children.

We, as mothers, are generally well-intended when we say our focus is our kids when we work that second job, or fight to keep that man around so there will be a male in the house. This is not always in the best interest of that little boy or girl that God has assigned to you in this life. It may not be good for your peace of mind, either. I was consumed with helping Delon break from his demons. Unfortunately, I was aloof to the fact that there were demons lurking and waiting for an opportunity to lure my unsuspecting little boy into an abyss called the LA streets. I had a son who needed me and a man who needed me. Actually, that man needed Jesus! I was entangled with him because of our history together, and truth be told, we loved each other. I allowed him back in my life, knowing it was a bad move. I had a habit of going back to the things that distract me from success.

The relationship with Delon was not good for me at all. I was physically in love and spiritually whipped because of him. I prayed always. I tried to "bring him to Christ," I wanted him to work and live right. I was tied to this man with shackles that I could not break. These shackles were not physical. They were spiritual and emotional. For this type of shackle, you need spiritual bolt cutters to break off the attachments you have picked up over your lifetime. Negative attachments, guilty feeling attachments, soul ties. My thoughts were on how I could change Delon. I wanted a good life with him, but I didn't realize that Delon's demon was an addiction to drugs, not other women. The drug addiction was stronger than anything you can imagine. His mind was altered, and he had no control of it. My mind was weighed down with worry and anxiety because I wanted Delon to change. I wanted to know where he was at all times. I wanted to be sure he was not messing with drugs. I was afraid he'd overdose or get arrested. I could not focus on school or work because I was wrapped up with Delon's life. These thoughts were spinning out of control. It was as if there was a relentless force trying to stop me from becoming what I believe I was supposed to be in life. If I had not regained control, my progress would have been paralyzed.

## Reflection

*Now that light has been shed over what a soul tie looks like; it is time to break it. I repeat, Break the soul ties. They are strongholds determined to keep you from moving up and out of a bad relationship.*

# Chapter 6

# Getting past the hurdles

*My soul was tied to him. I didn't realize I was shackled until I tried to leave.*

**MJEnvision1t**

Delon was one of many distractions that were relentlessly coming for me. Each one came harder and stronger just to set me back. I asked myself, *"girl what happened to getting your degree? What happened to making a good life for your son so that he can go to a good school in a nice neighborhood."* I had to stop, revaluate, and refocus on what I had envisioned for our lives. I had some decisions to make. I was doing ok; making a decent salary. I was making more than minimum wage and that better than most twenty-two-year-olds I knew. My baby was going on four years old, and my focus was on getting my four-year degree. *But, what about my baby boy?* He was subjected to all the stress I dealt with while working on my AA degree and dealing with a drug addict. He was the victim of my pain. I yelled at him for every little thing, and in some cases, just because he was not moving as fast as I wanted.

My mom was not in agreement with me as far as going to school and working. She thought I was taking on too much. She did not hesitate to let me know how she felt. Her pride and joy was her first-born grandson, Tyrell. She observed how I interacted with him and would quickly let me know when she thought I was not giving him enough attention. I was determined to get my four-year degree. I was making plans to transfer to one of the California State Universities once I completed junior college. She let me have it when I shared my college plans.

"Are you going to put that child through this all over again? Why don't you take a break? You need to spend time with that baby before you take on anything else." I can still hear my mom's voice trying to guide me in parenting. I told her that I was never going to get anywhere with just an AA degree. I have a future and it requires making money. I have to get my bachelor's degree. I was not letting the fact that I am a mom stop me. My mom was not trying to hear that. She went on to tell me that I needed to make time for my son. My pursuit was becoming unfair to him. I, with my flippant mouth, replied back to her asking, "what do you mean, not fair to him? I spend time with him. I help him with homework, I have him in T-ball. I am doing both, but I must get my education. I do not want to struggle and go through what you went through. You never finished because you had to work. I can do both. Education is everything for black people. We can't go far without it."

Mom so kindly answered back, "Nikki, I hear, but your son is going to suffer because you are not spending quality time with him. Do you love him?" I heard the seriousness in her tone.

"Yes, I love my son. That is why I am pushing so hard. I want him to have a good life. I cannot do that with just an AA degree. I would be stuck making a low income. I am pushing for six figures in my lifetime. I am pushing to retire at fifty-five, not sixty-five, or seventy. I want a lot for me and him."

I can remember that conversation so well. It is what I believed I had to do for myself. I was head-strong at an early age. I was even dealing with some anger toward my mom for leaving my dad, and for not planning for me to go to college. I had an idea in my head that I was supposed to have money for college when I graduated. I believed my parents were planning for me to go. I remember hearing my dad talk about a college fund when I was very young. Well, all of that went out of the window when my parents divorced. College was going to be paid for with student loans and my hard work if I wanted to go. I was on the honor roll most of my school years, but my GPA was a B average, so I did not get a full ride scholarship. I only knew what my counselors told me about obtaining funds for college and that was not much. I was pushed toward obtaining loans more than scholarships.

As a young girl, I could not understand why my parents were not as focused on college for me as I was. Now I get it, college costs. It seems out of reach for those living paycheck to paycheck. My goal was to go anyway and I made sure I got the funding to pay for it, even if it would take me twenty-five years to pay it back. I watched my mother go to school part-time while working and raising us after divorcing my father. I figured she tried, but it was hard since she had been out of school so long and had so much responsibility. I figured if I kept pushing while I was still young, I could get it done. I was afraid to stop then and go back later. I know of people who do that and never go back. I thought I could handle it all. I had a strong mother as an example. I remember my conversation with her, it was actually more like a monologue.

"Mom, you worked, went to college and raised us. It was a struggle for you, that is why you stopped at some point. I think that if you had finished college, you would have been making the kind of money you needed to keep out of the financial struggle. You would have been able to help me pay for college. That did not happen for me. I wanted college all my life. So, I pushed and pushed and worked, and did it. But, mom, an AA is not enough for me. You had help and it makes a difference. With your help, I can do it. Black people will never make it in this world unless they are educated. I do not want to be the stereotypical single mom who ends up on welfare for the rest of her life. I refuse to live in poverty. I am going to push myself as hard as I can to get my bachelor's degree. This is good for me and my son. He will have a role model to look up to. He will know the value of a college degree from my example. He will even get to go to a private school and it will not break me."

"Ok, Nikki", mom said. "You are so set on this. I will help you, but after this, you have to slow down."

"I know, mom and I thank you so much for always being there for me.", I said as I hugged her. I was not trying to be mean to my mom. I love her so much. She has been my best friend. She has been my rock and my loudest cheerleader, but I had misplaced anger toward her at times. It is not uncommon for children of divorce to be upset with one or the other parent. I read an internet article from Weinberger Law Group, a family law firm, that explains,

*"Children often target the "safe" parent during divorce because they know that parent will love them no matter what. If your marriage ended primarily due to your ex's behavior, your children's misdirected anger can make you feel depressed, guilty, and resentful."* [1]

If I were to psychoanalyze myself, I'd say that I pushed hard to avoid being upset with myself for getting pregnant right after high school. I was proving to myself that I could still meet my goals even though I had a baby. That attitude or way of thinking became almost toxic. It certainly impacted my child. I was well-intended, but I put so much stress on myself, that I started transferring it to him. I am thankful my mom was in my life so closely that she saw it, called me on it, and I was able to correct it before it had gotten out of control. I did not want to become abusive to my baby. I know there are many children who suffer from mental and physical abuse at the hands of their parents. I wonder if some of these parents were under pressure like I was, but did not have anyone to talk to that could help bring them out of it. I heard a message from Bishop TD Jakes at one of his worship services about parents who push hard to make sure their children have everything, but when it is all said and done, that is not what the kids really wanted or needed. He talked proudly of his grown children sitting at the table with him reminiscing about the moments they had together as a family. Not the stuff he bought them.

## Reflection

*What hurdles have you encountered on your journey? The short and easy or the tall and difficult? For me, it was my inability to prioritize the right things. I made some mistakes, like everyone else. It does not matter if you stumble. Get up, dust yourself off, learn what you need to improve upon.*

# Chapter 7

# The Player Who Caught Me

*An imprisoned heart cannot receive love from others because the mail stops coming into the facility. There is no one to answer telegrams of love sent by another, because the last guy took the key to my heart and put it on lockdown.*

MJEnvision1t

Here he comes *Mr. Playboy Extraordinaire*. I had been single for a while after I left Delon alone. Well, actually, he went to jail. Good for me, bad for him. I guess I still hadn't learned men very well. I was caught up, once again. Another cutie pie, roughneck, play boy-type came my way. Yes, he chose me, and I was feeling like, "yeah, that's right. I got Reggie chasing after me." I justified in my head that this time would be different, because this guy had a good job working in the aerospace industry, he had his own car, a sports car at that, and would not be asking to borrow mine. That has to be the best mix; a little rough around the edges, but working, and cute.

Reggie would pull up in the driveway of our apartment and call me from his car phone.

"Hey Nikki, come down stairs for a minute." I used to love the way he said that. It was something about his voice.

"Ok, give me a second," I'd reply. Then I would ask mom to watch Tyrell. She warned me to watch my heart with Reggie, but she did not stop me from seeing him.

"Sure, Nikki, go on." She replied.

"Thanks. I won't be long because I still have a paper to write for school." I walked down the stairs, excited and feeling giddy. I pretended to be cool when I got to the bottom of the stairs. "Hi, Reggie. What's up?" I tried to come off nonchalant.

"Hey, girl, not too much. What's up with you? He asked in his sexy voice, looking and sounding like the rapper Ice Cube.

"I have a paper to write. You know school is my priority", I responded wishing I could stop what I was doing and hang out with him.

"Are you writing it all night, or can you take a break to get something to eat?" He asked.

"Yeah, I think I can work that out," I said blushing.

"Ok, let me hit a few corners, then I'll call you before I come back. Alright?" He said with a bit of slang.

"Yes, that will work," I said.

He grabbed me like he always did and gave me one of his sexiest, wet kisses. I just wanted to melt right in his arms whenever he kissed me like that. But I had to get back to that paper.

"Ok, I will see you later tonight," I said, pushing him away playfully.

Reggie and I had an exciting, yet forbidden love thing going on. He would leave work for lunch and have me make him a chicken salad with apples and raisins. He was always looking for me to cook. That was the Texan in him. This west coast girl came from a Cajun family, so I knew how to put a few good meals together. Reggie was in love with me, and I was in love with him. It was unexplainable. When we met, his live-in girlfriend was pregnant with his daughter. I did not know this at the time. Honestly, when I met Reggie, I was not interested. I was looking at one of his friends. Reggie told me his friend was married, so I left that one alone. I would drive down Crenshaw Blvd, a popular street in Los Angeles, and as I got closer to my neighborhood, Reggie would just appear! At a corner or in the gas station, there he was. I wondered if he was following me. I even asked him, but he playfully avoided answering me. I thought it was sweet.

Reggie and I liked hanging out late at night on the weekends. He and I both worked during the day, and I had school. We would go to his friends' houses, take scenic rides along the coast, and for excitement, we hung out at the street races. This man was popular in the community. He had a magnetic personality, as well as jokes. He was a man of the hip-hop era. The music and the life-style is what he personified, to a degree. That is what had me so into him. When I found out he had a baby coming and that he was still living in the same house with his baby's mother, I wanted to leave, but felt too connected. He could tell me anything and I chose to believe it. I let him convince me that he was only there for the baby, but had checked out of the relationship long ago. I was so naive. The wake-up call happened when my mom answered a phone call from Reggie's baby's mother.

"Hello, yes, she lives here. Who is this? Kai? Oh, wait, what?" I could hear my mom's conversation in the kitchen. I went into the kitchen and asked her what was wrong. She covered the phone and told me Reggie's woman was on the phone. I took the phone and asked her what she wanted. She started telling me that she saw my number on the phone bill. So, Kai wanted to know who it belonged to. I noted that Reggie had a lot of female friends and asked why she had singled me out? Kai said my number showed up back-to-back many times, and it was the most calls he made. So, she figured something was going on. I told Kai I did not want to break up anything, and she needed to talk to him, not me. She told me that she had heard my name come out of his mouth and from others. She said he must really like me because the other women he had been with were nothing but whores. She was not worried about them, just me. I was a threat. I told her that they needed to work that out. I am not trying to be in that mix.

Later that night, Reggie came over. My mom and I had a conversation with him about what had happened. He told my mom he loved me and that Kai was his baby's mother. He was not sleeping with her anymore, but he had not moved out because he did not want his daughter to grow up without him. So, he did his thing, and she did her thing.

My mom pulled his card! She let him know that he can say that all day, but that you are still in that house and this woman is going through your phone bill, that relationship is alive and well. What he wanted was the best of both worlds in his mind. He wanted to be there for his daughter, but he wanted me, plus the freedom to talk to anyone else if he decided. He worked it his way for quite some time. I had to get tired before I could break free. I knew better. I was a believer in Christ, but I was still operating in my flesh, especially with Reggie. He was not a church-going man, but he would say, hey Nikki, I want to go to church with you. I'd say ok, let's go this Sunday or next, he would never be ready the day of. So yeah, he was playing games. I was so head over heels in love that I bought into whatever he said. Although my mom and brother knew the situation, the love this man showed me and them had us all giving him grace. It was one of the strangest situations I have ever experienced.

I knew better deep down, but it was just something about him. He knew what to say and how to say it. I would get so upset when I knew he was lying to me about something but would pretend like he didn't know what I was talking about. I would imagine throwing anything I could find at him just so he would know just how upset I was. Then I'd pause and think about the consequences if I did. I knew I would cry later, wishing I had never lost control. It was a wild ride on this forbidden love coaster. I say love because we really did love each other. It was apparent to all who knew us. It was just wrong. No sugarcoating. I had to find my way out of this web of entangled hearts: hers, his, and mine. It was not going to be easy.

### Reflection

*Is it possible to really love someone who you know that you can never be with, and that same person love you with just as much intensity, but cannot be with you? Or, is this just lust? Maybe so, or maybe not. Whatever your answer, someone gets hurt.*

# Chapter 8

# Thank you, Next!

*You can say thank you, next, when you have learned from your previous relationship. You are no longer bitter for the hurt, but appreciative of the lesson.*

It was hard for me to break loose from Reggie. He was genuinely in love with me and living with his child's mother. I had just been dating a guy, Kevin, who I later learned was engaged to be married. I found out from a relative of mine who worked with his fiancé. I never knew anything because he would have me over to his place, we went out with his friends, and he always called me or answered when I called him. He was a big spender and I enjoyed the places he took me for entertainment. This relationship was different than what I had with Reggie. Totally different scenarios in terms of the accessibility, and what I thought was transparency. Kevin lived his life the way he wanted. He did not put limits on himself. He was a man with big dreams at a young age. However, Kevin had an arrogant side. He carried himself with pride because he had achieved a lot financially at a young age. I do not think Kevin realized how condescending his words were to others when he talked about his accomplishments. He dressed well, had nice-looking cars, lived in a middle-class neighborhood, and loved fine dining. He was desirable. I knew women would be drawn to him, but I was not concerned. I had a lot of confidence in who I was. So, when I questioned him about the rumor of him having a fiancé, and he denied it, I believed him.

Unfortunately, his guilt got to him, and he eventually told me he felt terrible for lying about getting married. He started having second thoughts about going through with it. He tried to convince me that he really wanted me in his life. I was angry, disappointed, and just heartbroken. I went off on him for lying to me. He continued to pursue me, but I had dealt so long with Reggie and his playboy acting self that I did not have the energy for this one. Eventually, I stopped responding to his calls. I knew that continuing to engage in discussions with him would have me in a place I would regret. Kevin did get married, but quickly divorced. He and I became best friends later, actually we still are. He is a wonderful father, highly ambitious, and has a heart of gold. We were just not meant to be a couple.

My relationships with men kept me in prayer. First, I had to deal with my son's father and his drama, Reggie and his cheating ways, then Kevin and his lie. Between these men, there were others, but only short-term. I went out often just for fun. I had some good men who showed interest, but they were not exciting enough. My desire for fire in a relationship caused me to miss out on one or two who would have made great husbands. Once you've hit your head too many times, you muster up enough sense to stop moving in the same direction that is causing you to bump your head. I told myself not to waste any more time with men who did not love God. If they were in the street life, or hustling, I would no longer give them the time of day. That was my new rule and I was sticking to it. So, when I ran into Vernon, a man who was soft-spoken, a provider, and professed his faith in God, I was ready to try again.

I knew Vernon from high school. It had been a little over eight years since I last saw him. I was surprised to see that he was the man in front of me completing a transaction at the Bank of America teller window. Our eyes caught. We were surprised to see each other. The last time I saw Vernon, he was letting me down easy. I was four years younger than he, but in high school, the age difference seemed much wider. This man was different from the men I had allowed in my life. He was a small business owner and my high school crush. He was into real estate investing and owned a home security franchise. I had been carrying a torch for him since I was fourteen. I loved to watch him at work. My friends and I would walk up to Taco Bell after school to get an enchurito or a bean & cheese burrito. I guess I was stalking him. That smile! He reminded me of Blair Underwood by the eyes, skin-tone, and, again, that smile!

Vernon came back into my life when my son, Tyrell, was four. This was the second of three encounters since high school. I only dated him a short time, though. He was always leaving town. I remember one time, after we began dating and officially claiming each other as boyfriend and girlfriend, we were supposed to go out to dinner. Vernon called to say he had to leave town and we could not go. I asked him what came up so suddenly and all I got was nonsense. I was very experienced with men who lied, so I was able to smell a lie. I was upset and did not trust what he was saying. I went to his place to see what he was "really" up to. He was loading the jet skis with his "boys," and they were on their way to Lake Havasu, AZ. I demanded to know why I could not go. He gave me a bunch of lame excuses. A short while later, he got in trouble; those cars he was driving were hot. I don't know about the boat and the jet skis, but he was named in charges brought before the court for grand theft auto (GTA), he was allegedly the selling stolen exotic cars. *So much for the "nerdy" guy. How did I get into this again?*

Although I was disappointed, I did not break up with him right away. Vernon had me searching for lawyers. He connected me with his aunt and people he knew that had resources to help with his case. He ended up doing time, but not very long. While in prison, he made sure I had money to do what I needed. After a while, I realized the money did not matter. I did not want to live my life with another criminal-minded man. I was trying to live as a Christian but was still too carnal. I let my flesh rule and not the spirit. The carnal mind is limited by what it sees, tastes, or feels. That causes impulsive, sometimes, unwise decisions for those who have not learned to discipline their mind and body. It took me quite a few years to learn how to walk after the spirit and not after the flesh, as admonished in the Bible. That holy book is full of wisdom and insight. It is too bad many of us avoid reading or applying it. I would have avoided making so many bad choices if I had understood spiritual principles early on. It would take many more hard knocks before I would learn the lesson.

**\*\*\***

In my relationship journey, I was never really looking for love. Some people have a desire to be in love, or to be taken care of, or just to have a companion. Not me. I just went with the flow. If I met someone and accepted their invitation to go out, I would go with intentions of just having fun. If we had an attraction, I'd stick to it to see if it would work. I was not a "booty call" kind of person. I was going to church, so I was mindful of how I would be perceived. As hard as I tried to live "righteous," I kept falling into sexual relationships with men I thought were going to become my husband. I would wait a several months and in some cases a year before I let myself get intimate, so in my opinion, I was not very promiscuous. In the Christian faith, it doesn't matter if you occasionally had sex outside of marriage, it is still fornication and that is a sin. I justified it because the man I was with would act like or tell me we were getting married. All the while, he was playing games with something I felt was sacred.

Charles was one of those slick guys. He was a good-looking high school basketball coach. He kind of looked and had a demeanor like Kobe Bryant, R.I.P. We had lots of fun hanging out after work. I actually hung out with him at his parent's home. They seemed to like me. I met Charles through my neighbor's grandson. He coached him at Leuzinger high school, the same school Russel Westbrook attended. This young man had strong basketball skills and was being scouted. Unfortunately, he got caught up with the wrong crew and lost the function of his legs in a shooting. His coach, Charles, was talking to his grandmother just outside her apartment door when I passed by to go to my apartment. He looked away from her and stared at me as I walked by and headed up the stairs to my apartment. I heard him ask who I was. At some point, he passed his number to the grandson to give to me. I followed up with a call later. He asked me out, and I said yes.

We went out a couple of times. Charles was a joker; always making me laugh, or dancing around the house. He was like a big overgrown kid. He even brushed my teeth with his toothbrush while he brushed his. I would tell him he was gross and needed to stop playing so much. My son enjoyed being around him. I am sure it was because of his child-like behavior. We dated a few weeks before red flags started popping up. He would ask me to call him after work, and I would, but he would take his time to call me back. He gave me all kinds of reasons and excuses. I let it go because things come up and I did not want to seem like the insecure type of woman who had to question everything. He would end up calling me back soon enough. When he did, we would laugh and hang out as if nothing happened. Our connection was getting better and feelings were getting stronger between us.

One night after enjoying margaritas and Mexican food, we came back to my place and Charles stayed over. The next morning, my doorbell rang and it was Kevin! Kevin and I were done since I found out about the fiancé, so I was not expecting to see him. I cracked the door open slightly and asked what was up? Kevin must have noticed I was trying to keep him from entering the apartment because he tried peeping through the door while stating the obvious, "I just came to see my friend. "I held my guard at the door and asked him why he didn't just call first? He told me matter-of-factly that he was just in the area. I didn't buy it. I told him I just bet he was. Kevin pressed his luck and finally asked if he could come in. I did not expect that at all. My response was laughable, "Uh… well, I wasn't expecting--" I couldn't get my words out right. Suddenly, my son interjected by saying, "My mom has a man in her room, and it ain't you!" *Wow! Out of the mouths of babes.* I immediately instructed Tyrell to go back to his room. I was shocked. I was not expecting that from him at all. This showed me that children see and hear everything. They are perceptive and impressionable. So, we have to mind our behavior around them.

Kevin went on his way, and later, so did Charles. He turned out to be a jerk.

I saw Charles a few days after the uncomfortable situation in the parking lot of Ralph's grocery store, so I walked up to his car to say hello. As I approached, I noticed Charles had his head slightly turned toward the store's entrance and exit. It was as if he was looking out for someone. With each step I took, I could tell he was beginning to panic. *That was strange*, I thought to myself. I began to wonder what was going on. Finally, when I reached the driver's side of his car, he was apparently shaken. I asked what his problem was. He said he would call me later and asked me to just go on. I was like, wait, what? He had turned his head away from me and returned his focus toward the grocery store. He quickly turned back to me and, with anger in his voice, told me to go on, and he will call me later. I looked up, and a woman was coming to get in his car on the passenger side. It turned out that the woman was his wife.

Oh boy! Another cheater and liar. I took a break from men. I focused on my college degree and started a small business out of my apartment, writing business correspondence and resume's. I was taking my son to T-ball and trying to be a good mother. I went to church and took my little prince to a children's church. Life was good. I even bought myself a sports car. I felt blessed and so much better about the direction of my life. God was good to me, even a sinner who was saved by grace. I could make it through anything. I was relentless about making it in life and coming through each challenge glowing with resilience.

*Reflection*

*What lessons have you learned from past relationships? Have you made adjustments so that you will no longer repeat the pattern that leads you back into unhealthy relationships?*

# Chapter 9

# My Heart for Them, My Heart for Him

*Have you heard the phrase, Guard Your Heart? It is a biblical reference that says "Keep thy heart with all diligence; for out of it flows the issues of life" Proverbs 4:23. What matters most to us; how we treat ourselves and others, all come from the heart.*

MJEnvisionit

The year was 1994 and my little boy was almost seven years old. I had Tyrell enrolled in a Christian school and he would visit his dad during school breaks. His father was paying child support, so financially, we were okay. Life was shaping up pretty well for us. I decided to get out of the inner city and move to the suburbs. I wanted to get my son, and by this time, my little cousin away from big city life. I had taken guardianship of my cousin after his great aunt passed away. He was a fourteen-year-old kid with a loving heart. His mother and father did not participate in his life and I did not want to see him on the streets. Neither his sisters nor his parents would take him in, so I did. My goddaughters and my cousin all spent the summer with me and my son in our new town home in Upland, California. They enjoyed it. I was having a good time too. I made new friends in the community and would attend pool parties with the kids. I allowed myself to meet new guys, but my focus was on building friendships, not relationships. This new life without Reggie popping up was nice while it lasted.

A few months after I moved, Reggie reached out to see how I was doing. He asked to see me and I said no. He was relentless in his pursuit of me. He let it go that day, but a week or so later, he called again. He said he wanted to take a ride in my direction to come see how the boys and I were doing. He persisted until he wore me down. I gave him my new address. I moved to this quiet suburban community for its diversity and affordable apartments. I hoped that this environment would help my cousin, who later became my foster son, get focused in school and maybe pick up a sport. He also became a big brother to my then six-and-a-half-year-old son. I was only twenty-six at the time, and still a single mom. I was sure I could raise these boys on my own.

I was on top of their homework schedule, I made sure I knew where they were at all times. I was on top of school attendance. I made sure homework was done, etc. I knew right away when there was an issue with school for either of the boys. I did my best to expose the boys to people who were living right, working, love God and family, and lived well. I demonstrated the importance of a higher education as I continued working on my degree, while working and taking care of the boys.

At some point, I had begun talking to Reggie again. When I moved to Upland, Tyrell was about seven or eight years old. It had been a year since I decided to leave Reggie alone, again. I was no longer thinking about him until he called to say he was coming out my direction. That man drove all the way out to Upland to see me, nearly an hour east of Los Angeles, where he lived. No matter how many times he and I got into it over his living situation, or his "baby momma," we kept getting back together. He told me he missed me and that he was ready to move out of his baby's mother's house. He wanted me more than anything, let him tell it. I told him to leave me alone, but he persisted. I let him come visit and that was all it took. I got wrapped up in him when he came around. I was so head over heels into him. I never realized that our relationship was not good for the kids. We did not physically fight, but we would argue. That was not the issue. He had a great job, nice car, dressed well and smelled nice. You would think he was a good pick, but he was still living with his baby's momma, and he drank too much. I was entangled so deeply with this man. Our relationship was not good for me or the boys because this man could never be fully committed. I was foolish for thinking he could.

The boys were watching me in this so-called relationship. My cousin is grown now, but he had asked if I was still in touch with Reggie. He asked if he was still drinking. Then he brought up a time when he saw Reggie sloppy drunk. He would joke about it. Drinking to the point of being drunk is nothing to laugh about. We all know the dangers. The fact that it was funny to my cousin, who was much older than my son, made me wonder what he thought of me being in a relationship with a man like that. My cousin actually holds me in high esteem. He told me that he thought Reggie was a good guy, but he needed to slow down on the drinking. Reggie had a nice car, a good job, and a great personality. He was not violent nor did he talk crazy to me. I was one of the blessed ones because I was not in an abusive relationship with a drunk. The boys in my life never saw a man control me, or hurt me physically. They saw a strong black woman who was educated and worked very hard to give them a good life. Unfortunately, that was not enough. They needed a good male role model.

As mothers, especially young single mothers, we have to be aware of our choices who we allow in their lives. This is especially true for our sons. Just think about it, if you allow a man to disrespect you by calling you out of your name, yelling at you, or talking down to you, your sons may pick up the behavior and treat women the same way. On the flip side, if they are older, they may get so upset to see it that they may try to protect you. In doing so, they may even get into fights with the man who is treating you badly. Mothers would do well to find good men to mentor their sons. Whether the man is one you are dating or a friend, check his character and see if he would be the one who you want your son to learn from. If he is not that guy, then you should rethink your relationship. If you can get your son into sports or other activities that will keep him from having idle time, and will get him in an environment where he can learn from "good men", that will make parenting boys as a single mother much easier. Life is overwhelming for us as adults, our children should not have to be exposed to, or take on our issues.

My cousin ended up going from house-to-house, and later living with me because his mother did not think about him or his siblings when it came to fulfilling her desire to have a man in her life. She was not ready to be a mother. She prioritized her love life over her children and did not raise her children herself. Her daughters were raised by their father's family and her son, lived with his great aunt before coming to me. I reached out to his father for help since he lived in the same area I had moved to, but he kept making excuses for why he could not be there for his son. I tried my best to show him the right way to go, but ultimately, he moved in with his older sister. He was about sixteen at this time. He eventually started running with a local street gang, and got involved in the criminal justice system. He was looking for male leadership and he was dealing with abandonment. This is a common, yet unfortunate story for quite a few black boys in America. We lost contact for a while, but reconnected via telephone a couple of years later. He loved me like a mother and loved my son like his little brother. He had a loving heart, but life dealt him a hard blow. Because of his gang affiliation, he ended up getting a gang enhancement in a case he caught that to this day he maintains his innocence. I keep him in my prayers and I have been seeking legal assistance. The matter is ongoing. His parents have not lifted a finger to help, nor do they visit him. Our youth do not always require discipline. Some kids are acting out because they are lacking love in their lives.

### Reflection

*Why do we keep bumping our heads against a brick wall when we know we are going to get hurt?*

# Chapter 10

# His Relentless Pursuit

*I thought I was finally free from him, but his relentless pursuit of me propelled me into a space that almost had me believing a lie.*

**MJEnvisionit**

In my relentless effort to free myself from Reggie, I opened my heart to possibilities with someone else. I met a man who I thought could finally satisfy my relational needs. That was TL. My relationship with TL was good initially, but short-lived. I was struck by his good looks, his tall frame, and the way he carried himself. He came off classy with sex appeal. He lived near my family and was part of the Lemert Park District. This was an area that had lots of culture and artistry. Quite a few people in the entertainment industry lived in and around the area. I was caught up in the vibe of it all and because TL was attached to it, I was in awe of him too. He favored Idris Elba and Blair Underwood; just hands down a handsome man. I was so caught up in that. I did not know about his dark side until much later. I was twenty-eight now and had gained a few years of experience with men, but I never lost the attraction I had for the wrong kind of guy. *Why is that? What is it in our flesh that desires the very thing that is not good for us?*

I thought TL was good for me! I would come over to his apartment after work and cook dinner for us. We would go to the laundry mat and he would teach me how to fold clothes his way. He was meticulous. He knew how to fold perfectly. He had an older son around seven or eight years old and a younger son around two years old. He spoke well of his sons and their mothers. I got the impression he was a good father. He was very into his youngest son. That little boy was a cutie! Both were. He also had another son who had been killed a couple of years prior. I do not know the story, but I he talked briefly about him. He seemed upset more about the choice his son made to live the lifestyle he lived that brought his demise. I never heard sadness in his voice for some reason. I should have sensed that to be a red flag waving around. In retrospect, it seems as if TL was trying to push blame on his son for his death. I wonder if he was feeling bad for not being in his son's life. TL was good at making a matter appear to be someone else's fault. I still did not see violent tendencies in him. My uncle is the one who first told me to be careful with TL. He shared how he caught him arguing then putting his hands on his son's mother. He told me that he let TL know in no uncertain terms that if he put hands on me, he'd be handled. I kept my uncle's words in the back of my mind as I continued seeing TL.

We kept seeing each other for nearly a year. During this time, I learned so much more about TL. He was not all that the package presented him to be. He carried himself with a lot of class, on the surface. His circle was with those in entertainment. He was diverse in his experiences and I liked that. I was trying hard to break from the usual. I found out later, that I had not broken from the usual at all. This guy actually moved in the same circles as one of my uncles. They both shared a dark past that involved drugs and organized crime. Not at all the life I wanted to be part of. I would ask, *"Lord, why?"* I could not understand why I was continuing to attract men who were connected with a street life-style. *Was it the idea of living on the edge?* Maybe it reminded me of my childhood with my adoptive father. He is the only dad I knew as a child. His family was the only family I knew and loved dearly. It was a large family of 8; 7 boys and one girl. My aunt was the baby of the siblings. All were good-looking men, with a street-life edge. I think I was trying to replace my dad and the lifestyle I grew up with. I was doing this through the kind of men I was drawn toward. My uncles and my dad spent time in the military, had good jobs, but at some point, my dad and a couple of my uncles began to teeter on the dark side, mostly as a result of "opportunities" presented by their little brother. He was the youngest of my uncles, and his lifestyle was filled with criminal activity. He was the uncle who moved in the same circle as TL.

One day, during pillow talk with Jamar's father, I learned of his connection to my uncle who was living dangerously. It was the past. As long as that was the case, I thought I should not have to worry about the police bursting into his apartment looking for something illegal, or some drug dealer looking to collect on a deal. He was in church now. I actually believed he'd be good for me since he was a Christian and went to church. I was young, so I had not yet come to realize that just because a man went to church, that did not make him a great guy. I had not learned the lesson that humans are flawed and prone to error. I learned the hard way, yet again.

I was with TL when his father took ill. He asked me to ride with him to the hospital to see his terminally ill father. When we arrived, his father appeared week and barely able to speak. It became apparent to me that TL had an agenda in that hospital room. He was not just there to pray over or check on his dying father. He was trying to find out if he had a will. He tried his best to get his father to write down what he was leaving to his kids. He even wrote some words on the paper and tried to make his father sign it. He was actually trying to get material things and money from his father through manipulation. He was taking advantage of him on his death bed. I was beginning to see the potential he had to be heartless. It was only when I found out I was pregnant did his level of evil fully come to light for me. He literally began to act like he despised me. Honestly, I was at the point of almost despising him. He was not a good person at all. His mother didn't trust him. He was not close to his family. He showed up for the barbecues and family gatherings, but to me that was just for show, or to get the good food they were cooking. I was not happy with him an I was so glad to be done with the relationship. I could raise my son without him. I had experience already. And, I had Reggie in the background of my life. He was still lingering.

I don't know if it was wishful thinking or if it could have been true, but I began wondering if this child was really Reggie's., I thought I was through with him, but he never stopped chasing me. I wanted to be done, but I gave in one day. Another baby on the way ten years after my first born. I have my four-year degree, now and am getting ready to close on my first home, before the age of thirty! Yes! I made this my goal, and I am achieving it. This journey has been tough, but by the grace of God I am doing it. All by myself. No man to help me. I chose to be the best me I can be with or without a man. I never required validation. I never needed a man to accomplish my goals. I have been in love. I have tried relationships after relationships, but not because I needed a man. So, in having this next baby, I did not get all in my feelings when his father kicked me to the curb. I was still in love with Reggie, but did not realize it until I noticed I was not as broken as I should have been with the father of my child telling me he was done with me. The timing of my intimate moment with Reggie, and the last time I was with TL was very close. Based on the ultra sound due date estimate, my baby could have been Reggie's.

I was about 97% sure it was, at least that is the probability that I pulled out of my head when he asked. I was keeping my fingers and toes crossed that he was the father. TL and I were not working out and he made it clear he wasn't going to be involved.

Reggie and I had continued with this on and off, hot and cold relationship for nearly nine years at this point. He was relentlessly pursuing me, but continuously hurt me. If you let him tell it, I hurt him. We were a forbidden love that just could not stay away from each other. We took long breaks thinking we were done, but a year later, we would get right back together. He'd call me just to get on my case about why I was wrong for not trusting him or not believing he loved me. The phone would ring and I'd answer to hear him say, "Hey Nikki, you know I love you. How could you? After all we have been through. Girl, you know how I feel about you. Why would you get with this clown?" He was talking about TL.

Reggie lived right down the street from me, and his brother lived across the street, so Reggie could see who was coming or going. I would snap back at him asking what nerve he had to ask me "how could I?" He had nerves, especially when he had been living with his daughter's mother all these years while at the same time telling me he loved me. Again, I say, *the nerve of him! Talking about I just need to give him time. Really dude?* Time should have been up long ago. I started to realize that I was a big fool. I was crazy to keep waiting for him. I got tired and decided to move on. I thought TL and I were going to work, but the relationship was dying on the vine. It did not last long. By the time Christmas of 1996 came around, TL and I were drifting apart. He was not focused on me and I could feel it. By this time, I was already pregnant, but I did not know it. I still had my monthly cycle. I was taking birth control pills, but would miss a day or two once in a while.

I had no idea Reggie would come see me on Christmas Eve. He just showed up and when he did, that man was all up in my ear telling me the things I love to hear. I was vulnerable, and it was Reggie. So actually, I slipped up with him. We were no longer together, but the passion between us was easily ignited once we were in each other's presence more than a few minutes. When Reggie would bring up his disappointment in me for having Jamar by someone else, I would remind him that we were no longer in a relationship. He would rebut and say, "Yeah, yeah, yeah, it doesn't matter. I never got over you. I will never stop loving you. I have always told you that." I would then remind him that he never left his daughter's mother like he said he would. He came back with the same words he had been saying for quite some time; that he could not leave his daughter. He never wanted another man to raise her. That was his story for a few years now.

He'd go on about why I should have given it more time. He would tell me how hurt he was when he saw a guy, I was dating drop me off or leave my apartment, I would remind him of the many times I saw him pass by me on the road with a different woman in the car. My question back to him was *how many times have I waited for you to come over or take me out, but only to find out you kicked it with someone else?* Reggie was just a player. I was initially worried about him not leaving his situation, but I had a bigger concern with him messing around with women in general. I would argue with him that he did not love his child's mother, or me. I told him to get out of here with that noise.

He was all talk, no action. He finally got the message and left. I tried to hold back my tears as I closed the door behind him, but failed.

I felt the warmth of my first teardrop roll down my face as I stood wondering why I allowed this man back into my life. *Why was I even having this conversation with him?* I needed God more than ever, now. I knew no other way to get past the pain of heart break. I was already attending Bible study at church. I never stopped going to God in prayer, even in my moments of carnality. I was trying to live right, but my flesh was weak. My sin was my heart for a man who could talk a good game. This time, I was a little older and wiser. I was getting closer to God and I was tired of the drama in my life. That made it easier for me to tell Reggie to go. On top of that, I was being distracted from reaching the goals I set for myself. I was twenty-nine and finally getting close to graduating with my bachelor's degree! I did not need all of the distractions that came with relationships, even worse, with a relationship like the one with Reggie. I had to get my life back on track. I would soon be giving birth to another son and I was living in an apartment with roommates. I wanted to raise my children in a home, so I had a goal of becoming a homeowner before the age of 30. I could no longer waste time with distractions. I became even more determined to reach my goals.

### Reflection

*Have you looked at a woman with young children and wonder where the father was? Did you find yourself ready to judge her? Have you stopped to think that just maybe she is not a whore, or "fast-tale" woman? Instead, she may have fallen in love with the wrong guy? We don't know the story of others. Instead of judging, let's find out if a sister needs a little help or encouragement.*

# Chapter 11

# It's a Boy!

*There are far too many black boys being raised without a good male role model. As a result, too many young men and boys seek leadership from those who appear to have power and respect. Unfortunately, the power and respect are demonstrated by street culture.*

**MJEnvisionit**

*What a beautiful baby boy! 9-lbs, 11-ounces.* Another C-Section. This time, I not only brought home a baby, but I brought home a very annoying and dangerous disease, diabetes, and did so as a single parent. Diabetes made me drop several pant sizes. It kept me off kilter. I snapped at anything and I did not know why. This disease is awful. People did not understand how I could be diabetic because I was so skinny. I went from 165 pounds during pregnancy to 145 pounds almost immediately after I gave birth. For my height and body frame, I looked sick. Almost anorexic. I was going through uncontrolled diabetes. My sugar levels were everywhere. One of the symptoms is rapid weight loss, along with excessive thirst. I was told it would go away after having my son since it was gestational. I really hoped that it would.

I brought my baby home to a small village of women ready to help me; my roommates. The apartment I lived in was the same one that I had moved to with my mother eight years earlier, when my eldest was two and a half years old. It was the same apartment that my son spoke those sharp-tongued words to Kevin when Charles had stayed overnight. My mom had remarried and moved in with her new husband when I was about eight months pregnant with Jamar. My cousin and a lady that one of my friend's recommended became my roommates. The lady was from the Ivory Coast. I loved learning of her culture. She was studying nursing and was very helpful with cooking, cleaning, and with my little one. Both she and my cousin loved caring for my baby boy. It takes a village is so true. I was happy to have mine. My cousin loved babies so much and every second she could get to hold my new bundle was a joy for her. I felt bad when I would go into her room and ask her if I could have my baby. It was kind of funny, too.

The day I told my roommates I was buying a home and would be moving was hard for all of us. I did not want to lose them because of the bond and the help they so graciously provided. The house I was buying was not very large. It was just big enough for Tyrell and Jamar to share a room and for me to have my own. I must say, in retrospect, I should not have moved then. I did not know the issues and the dangers that was going to attach itself to the decision I made to buy that first house. I also did not think about the fact I would be raising another child alone, again.

*Welcome to our new home my beautiful baby! Momma has a place for you and your big brother to grow and play! No more apartment living. We have a yard, a play area, and a dog!* I spoke to my little guy with so much joy. I was so excited about the results I saw manifest in my life. I moved in faith and high confidence that I could by a home without a husband. I did not need a man. I could do it on my own. Well, not totally on my own, I had my heavenly Father looking out for me. Praise be to God! Life is improving, but that diabetes was giving me a hard time. I dropped down to a size five in clothing, when I was normally between a size ten and twelve before my pregnancy. I didn't mind the weight dropping at first. I thought I was looking pretty good until my mom, and Reggie expressed concern. I didn't know that people were wondering about my health because I was so thin. On top of that, I would be on the verge of passing out because of low blood sugar episodes. I tried to keep sweets in the house, or in my purse to avoid passing out. My eldest didn't understand how dangerous my situation was. I remember going into the kitchen on a few occasions to treat a low blood sugar episode but there was barely anything left. I recall one night getting upset with him about it. He was ten years old, and sweets were his thing. To this day, Tyrell loves sweets. At that time, however, I could care less about his sugar fixation, I wanted, no, I needed him to leave my stuff alone.

I was angry and feeling lightheaded when I started yelling, "Tyrell, my sugar is dropping. Get me some candy quickly." I was scared and upset when he replied that there wasn't any more candy. "What! My blood sugar is dropping I need something sweet. Are the Pop Tarts in there?" My voice was becoming louder and harsher.

"No Mom," he replied guiltily.

"What? Tyrell, what have I told you about touching my stuff! My sugar is dropping too low and I am sweating. This is not good. Why can't you leave my stuff alone?" I would scold him about this issue more often that I believed I should have. I finally found something sweet enough to raise my blood sugar. I sat for a few minutes, then the baby started crying. I needed to get to him, but I was still light headed. I asked Tyrell to help me. He picked him up and gave him his bottle. Tyrell loved his little brother, and I know he loved me, but our relationship was feeling strained. Partly because Tyrell was getting older and I was always busy with work or the new baby. I didn't realize this back then, but I see all of this in retrospect. I can see that I was handling my new child a little better than my first one. This child bonded with me so well. He was my shadow well into the end of elementary school. My first son and I did not hit it off too well at first. I tried to nurse him; but he did not latch on well. When I had Tyrell, I was focused on school and career, with some dating in between. I was stressed!

My life, then, left very little time for my firstborn. Oh, what a wild harvest I would soon reap.

***

My son, Tyrell, loved his little brother and did not mind helping. He changed his diaper, fed him and gave him his bottle. He was a big help. It ended when his dad decided he wanted Tyrell to live with him. I have heard people say a woman cannot teach a boy how to be a man. Those words played in my head as I contemplated my decision to let him go. I wanted my son to be with his father so he could learn from a man. I wanted him to get the teachings, the structure, and the discipline his father could provide. The decision was a hard one because that was my little boy. He had been with me since he was born. I was the one who took him to elementary school on my way to work. I helped him with homework and went to open house to meet is teachers.

As I thought about how much time I would spend with my son as a single parent, I realized that I could use a break. It was time for his father to do his part. *Why should I shoulder it all by myself?* Yes, I would miss seeing his handsome face every day, but I needed his father to be a good influence and role model in his life. With good intention and a belief that this would be the best move for my son, I said yes to his father when he asked for him. My little boy was off to live with his dad for middle school and I was going to focus on Jamar at home. His father was not involved in his life for the first few years. He did not provide financial, physical, or emotional support for his son. I took care of everything for Jamar.

I signed up with the Westchester YMCA. This was in an upper middle-class area of Los Angles, so it had strong funding. The facility was beautiful. The location was desirable. That is what drew me to it. I loved the two pools; one for lap swimming and the other for children and families to splash around. I did that with Jamar. We had a great time. I later saw that the YMCA had youth basketball. I wanted Jamar to join a basketball or T-ball program so he would be around men and little boys his age. At first, he was too young to play on a team, so the YMCA coaches made him a mascot. He showed interest in basketball very early. I was so proud of my baby boy. That kid could handle a basketball at two and a half years old! In my head, I just knew he was born to be an NBA star, and if not that, he'd surely go to college on a basketball scholarship.

I put a lot of time and love into this little boy. He was adorable, so it was easy for anyone to fall in love with him. His cousins offered to watch him while I ran errands or just to give me a break. My aunt and my friends offered to watch him as well. It was not hard to get a sitter for Jamar. He also made an impression on, guess who? Reggie. Jamar was a little over two years old and Reggie was still there. He never did completely leave my, or Jamar's life. He was at the hospital when I gave birth to Jamar. We had not resolved the issue of whether or not he or TL was Jamar's father at the time I gave birth. Reggie wanted to be his dad, so he made sure he was in his life on day one. We both felt deep down that he was not. We never took a DNA test for fear of confirmation he was not Jamar's father. Reggie would come visit him at my house and dribble the basketball with him. He would rock him to sleep when he was a newborn. His presence in Jamar's life was consistent for about three years. Suddenly, Reggie started backing off. I assumed he was back with his daughter's mom. I really didn't care as much as I had before. I was working hard, I now had two boys, and I had become numb to heartbreak. There was not much Reggie could do to upset me anymore.

As Reggie and I drifted apart, I began dating again. I had really good men come and go. Mostly because I had trouble falling in love again. I would push men away because I stayed so busy that I rarely made time for them. I dated a guy who had his own plumbing business, but found out he was an ex-drug dealer and had served a lot of time in jail. He became pushy and began doing things to my house without asking. When I confronted him, he said that my house was his house. He started meeting people late at night on my front porch. When I asked what he was doing, he said a friend was in a little trouble and needed a little cash, so he let her come by to get it. I did not believe him. I became suspicious. I really thought he was back into dealing drugs. I was into another relationship with a man with street ties. Little at a time, I noticed him becoming possessive of my house. He moved my furniture out back and brought his in. Then cut my blinds to fit his salt water aquarium. I had come home from work and this was all done. I made the mistake of giving him a key. Now I had to get him out. I knew just how to do it; I called one of my uncles. I let him know what was going on and he let me know I did not have to worry; he and the rest of my uncles would get him out. They did, too. I took another break from dating after that, it was about two years before I let anyone else into my life.

**\*\*\***

While my eldest was still living with his father, his little brother was growing and becoming very active at the YMCA and doing well in pre-school. I was moving up where I worked, and was starting to look toward getting my master's degree. I never let go of my educational goals. I had them on hold while I focused on Jamar. I learned a hard lesson when I tried to work and do school with Tyrell as a young child. I was very happy to hear that Tyrell was doing well in school. He was on the honor roll and in the eighth grade by this time in our lives. I was excited that soon, my mom, Jamar, and I would be flying out to watch Tyrell graduate from middle school. Tyrell had grown to be a smart, responsible, and handsome teenager. I was glad he had the experience of living with his father. Soon he would be off to high school and making even more progress.

His father and stepmother were gracious hosts to me and my family while we visited in celebration of Tyrell's accomplishment. We ate well and took lots of photos together. His stepmother, who had issues with me before we ever met in person, was actually accepting of me. She even held Tyrell's baby brother and discussed how she loved having my son live with them. I felt like things had gotten better between us and I was glad for my son's sake. It was hard for my mom and I to leave Tyrell, but she and I had to get back to southern California so we could be ready for work the following Monday. I kissed my son and let him know how very proud I was of him. I was looking forward to him continuing to do well in high school. I had no idea what was coming a few months down the road.

# Chapter 12

# A Relentless Fight for My Son

*Sometimes a boy doesn't need his behind whipped, sometimes he is just in need of love from his father. A boy should be able to have confidence that his dad will protect him from harm and danger. If he does not get that assurance, he may act out in misunderstood antics, even menace, or rage.*

**MJEnvisionit**

I was back in Los Angles, enjoying being a mom to Jamar, taking him to basketball practice, working out at the YMCA, and living life without the stress of a relationship. I had begun working out to control the diabetes and it was working okay. I had dropped down to a size five in dress size and loved it. My career was moving in the right direction. I wish I could say the same for Tyrell. After attending his graduation from middle school, and having a few good conversations with his dad and step mother, there was no way I could have imagined what was to come a couple of months down the road. I was headed into a battle for him. This battle was spiritual and physical. The mental trip his father put me and my son on was uncalled for. The blame game that started once Tyrell began going in the wrong direction was hurtful. I was in a fight for my eldest son and it was not going well. The impact of decisions I and my son's father made were immeasurable. We thought we were doing the right thing. I believed sending a boy to live with his father was the best thing a single mother could do. His father thought showing military style discipline was what a male child needed. Although on the surface, these are necessary in child rearing, there were missing ingredients; quality time, a listening ear, and understanding. Tyrell's dad and I were hard workers. We both wanted a lot in life, so we pursued hard. His father

79

had bought a home after discharging from military service. He also started a business. I wanted my son to be around him because he could show him how to be a man. Unfortunately, it did not work out the way I had hoped. His father called to tell me he was sending him back home to live with me. This was the night before school was to start in my area.

He was fourteen years old and his little brother was four at this time. I was not prepared for my eldest to come back. The back story from his dad was that Tyrell ran away and he was not going to put up with his behavior. I could not believe that he was telling me this. His father kicked him out of house for running away. On top of that, he only gave me a day's notice to meet him at the airport and find a school. This was the beginning of a new set of drama. I had to make adjustments quickly. School started on Monday and I was picking him up on Sunday. I would have to call in late to work, or maybe off from work so I could get him enrolled. I did not understand how this could be happening so suddenly. It did not make sense to me.

In retrospect, Tyrell was never truly happy living with his father. I still remember when my son called me upset with his father.

"Mom, I want to come home.," hurt dripped from his young voice. I asked him why and he said to me in such a sad voice, "Daddy does not care about me. He doesn't spend time with me. He just uses me to do his work."

"Oh Tyrell, I don't believe that. He loves you. He just shows it differently. I am sure he is just giving you responsibilities around the house to prepare you for life."

"I don't like it here. Every time I do or say something he doesn't like; he says I get that from you. I want to come home and be with you and my little brother."

I reiterated, 'Tyrell, you are doing so well. You are an honor roll student. You are active at the gym and staying in good shape. That comes from being in a different environment; one where you have a man in charge."

Tyrell was not backing down. He continued trying to convince me why I should let him come home to me. "Momma you don't understand. I don't think my dad loves me."

Ok, I will talk to him", I replied. So, I went ahead and gave his father a call. His new wife answered. I went ahead and let her know why I was calling. *Why did I do that?* I was called everything in the book. I was lying. I was putting words in Tyrell's mouth. I was a drama queen. I even wanted his daddy back. *What a twisted mind?* I asked them to listen to what Tyrell was expressing and they flipped the script on me. This man actually ended up taking me to court for child support. This was a bit crazy because he still owed me over $6,000 in back support. We had an agreement that since he owed so much that he was not going to ask me for anything once I let Tyrell come live with him. Once again, there was no reasoning with them. And this was not the first blow up between us.

Before this, my son's stepmother attacked me verbally during the ninth month of my pregnancy. I received a call from her cursing me out for asking my son's father for money to help me buy him a bedroom set. She accused me of being a gold digger and just wanting the money for myself. She even cursed the God I serve. She was awful. When I tried to talk to his father, he blamed me for upsetting his woman. *The woman called me and cursed me out, but I upset her. Go figure.* Anyway, this situation turned out to be just one more thing to brutally and negatively impact our son's life.

I guess it was wishful thinking when I got excited about Tyrell graduating from middle school and continuing with his father for high school. I now had to find a high school in one day. For some that is easy because each neighborhood has a public high school. I did not want Tyrell going to school in the neighborhood. I checked with family and chose a school where his cousins were attending. It was West Angles Christian Academy. That was a sought-after private school. I told Tyrell's dad to send me the money for tuition, then got him enrolled within two days of school starting. I wanted him to have the best education. I tried hard, but unfortunately, I still had to work. I worked extremely hard because, you see, I was now a homeowner.

I had two kids, and I had to pay day care fees, plus private school fees. I had help from Tyrell's father, but not from Jamar's. I did not require a lot of financial help, I made things work, but I certainly needed a strong male role model for my sons. Young men growing up at the beginning of the hip-hop era, without fathers in the home, or without a good man in their lives, were vulnerable to gang culture.

I tried all I could to keep that lifestyle away from my sons. We did much of our activities in the higher income communities so they could be far away from bad influences. I reached out to men in my family to spend time with them, but the time spent was minimal. They had their own lives and just could not be consistent with mine. Over a period of a few months, things started changing with Tyrell. He was rebelling against my rules. He started smoking weed and hanging out with friends who lived in some of the roughest parts of Los Angeles. I threatened him with military academy. I called his dad for help, but that turned into an argument about who was at fault. I was not able to focus on work anymore because I was concerned about where he was going after school. I tried to get him to see what he was doing to me and to himself. I told him

effective immediately, he was going to the SCORE after school program.

"But mom! I don't want to go." He was hoping that would stop me.

"You don't have a choice. I will pick you up from there after I get off of work. Oh and on Tuesdays, I am taking you to Bible study so you can get with positive kids your age. I am changing my schedule at work so I can pick you up daily." I said emphatically. I had a plan to get Tyrell back in line. It worked for a little while, but my job became more demanding. I was not able to get off work in enough time to pick up my son. I started allowing him to catch the bus home; he was fourteen now. I was nervous, but had no choice. Everyone I knew had jobs and could not help me with after school pick up duty.

The neighborhood where I bought my first house, became the neighborhood of my worst nightmare. I did not know there was a gang presence that was lurking around the corner when I first moved in. I moved there when my son was going on eleven years old, so I did not hear much about what was going on. I was working and he was in private school. Later, he went to live with his father for middle school. I was hearing things, but it was not hitting close to home for me. By the time my son came back to live with me, things had gotten worse in our neighborhood. Kids were getting shot not too far from us.

This was the worse time for his father to lift his hands from Tyrell. He needed the love and guidance of his father at this critical age. I was not enough. I let Tyrell have friends, but I wanted to know their parents and where they lived. I did not want him hanging around knuckleheads. I met a couple of parents. They were living in two-parent homes, so I felt a little more comfortable. Later, Tyrell started hanging with boys who were a little rough. They were drinking and smoking weed. I talked to Tyrell about the choices he was making and that he needed to go back to his other friends and leave these guys alone.

He was too far gone, but I did not know that. Tyrell began sneaking out at night when I was asleep. I put him in a local Sheriff's program, basically a Boot Camp to deter young boys from getting into gang or criminal activities. Tyrell's Boot Camp coordinator, a deputy Sheriff – thought that a local gang had a serious hold on him because he was not following the program. The Sheriff's had a hard time breaking him from his behavior. I remember the scary conversation the Sheriff had with me concerning Tyrell. My heart dropped when he said to me, "Ma'am, you have to start looking into his personal stuff to see if you notice any gang related items. Something is not right. He seems to be a pretty decent kid, but he is struggling with something. He wants to do right but something has got a hold of him."

The deputy Sheriff was right. I found things. I questioned him; he was only defensive. He started running away. He was starting to take things from his little brother and making us both upset. I hated seeing the hurt in Jamar's eyes. He loved his big brother, like his big brother used to love him. I am sure he still did, but he was preoccupied with the streets. He would take his little brother's things out of the house to sell them. He was getting high. He moved into the garage without my permission. Oh, what a fight between mother and son that soon ensued.

*Tyrell where are you? Why is my couch in the garage?*

He defied me, he started to push me away from him when I reached out to knock some sense into him. He lifted the futon as if he wanted to throw it at me. He socked the mirror and shattered it. I called the police. He was out of control. I had to do a citizen's arrest on my own son. This kid was lashing out. He was suffering. *Where was his father? Where was his uncle? Where were the male role models?*

This hurt me to see and be a part of the anguish my firstborn was going through. I did not know how to fix it for him. It was a job for a strong father or father-figure. Sisters, please do not minimize the role of a man in your man-child's life. It is very important. Do not over discipline and by no means take a hands-off approach. The time out stuff is crap when you have a child who has learned to manipulate his way through. Corporal punishment is not the answer when a child is truly experiencing self-hate, rejection, and just not feeling loved. You have a time bomb on your hands and you had better recognize it. Often, we as a people say just beat his blankety-blank-blank, he'll act right. Maybe so, or at least for the moment. But what if all you do is beat his behind, but never show him love? Or, what happens if you never take time to talk to him to know what is in his head? All that discipline means nothing in a scenario like this. You may have a kid who fears you, but he hates your guts and cannot wait for you to get out of his life. When you have that situation, you are dealing with a child who will run to anyone who will listen or who will give him attention. My son was missing love from his father. He knew I loved him, but it was not enough. I was not able to give him the amount of time or attention he needed. He knew that his mom worked so hard and went to school, but he did not understand that I was under a lot of pressure. The truth is that he should not have had to suffer. He did not have to be subject to that, nor to a father who showed him mostly authority and little love.

84

This kid came back to live with me, his momma, but there was no male figure to show him how to navigate his feelings or life. His uncle always had an excuse. This kid would give anything to be with his uncle. He never complained when his uncle said, "Sorry, I can't kick it with you today." He just suffered in silence. He called his big cousin, but he had a new lady, so he could not kick it with his little cousin. Who was waiting for this young man, but the local street gang? This became his new family. He loved his momma, but momma was not a man. I did not know how to intervene effectively. The gang problem was getting worse. I was afraid of losing my eldest son and now my preschooler, soon to be kindergartner. I decided to prepare the house for section 8 and start looking for a renter. I had work to do to the house to get it ready for a section 8 inspection. It was going to take a little more money, so I had to save up for the repairs. This would make us have to stay a little while longer. I wanted to save my son, so I wanted to get the place rented and move on for Tyrell's sake.

# Preying on the Little Prince

*Coddled by mama and disciplined by dad*
*This little prince struggled to get here, it was somewhat sad*

*There was a dark force that wanted to stop him from coming forth*

*But there was a light, with power and might that held back the cord*
*It was Mamma's prayers that she sent to the Lord*

*He's here now, love rained from above.*
*And brought him out, and placed him in the shelter of a mother's love,*

*He's growing up and making moves not realizing the world in which he's*
*living*
*is not as kind or nor is it forgiving.*

*As he steps through life and he looks around*
*trying to figure out what fate abounds*

*He sees signposts directing him this way.*

*And that way; he stands confused,*

*What voice is he supposed to listen to?*

*They are luring him to a playground that seems so cool,*
*But little does he know it is a cesspool*

*He stops and looks back at his Momma, hoping for approval*

*But she shakes her head no, and he stands contemplating*
*Mamma knows best, there was something sitting and waiting*

*I found out the hard way the sting of its bite had me screaming in the night*

*I should never have strayed from the shelter of my mother's love*

# Chapter 13

# Relentless Trials of Life

*When the enemy won't stop, you can't either. You must get bold and put on the whole armor of God. Get the sword of the spirit because the weapons of our warfare are not carnal. This is not a physical battle, it's a war going on in the heavenlies and we better get equipped so we can win with Christ*

MJEnvision1t

February 17, 2002, Jamar asked me to watch him play basketball outside in the back. I could not move from my bed. The fight that Tyrell and I had last night has worn me out mentally. I felt so hurt behind Tyrell. He acted like he hated me. It was almost as if he was punishing me for something. I couldn't understand why he fought me on getting things done around the house. I felt like I had given him so much. I tried not to be too hard on him about the phone or going out with his friends, but he said I was over protective. How in the world can he call me over protective? I just recently allowed him to go to a teen night club with a few of his friends. I really did not want to do this, but I did. I did the mommy thing. I dropped the kids off and picked them up. I made sure he had enough money to call me when the party was over. This is a kid who, in my mind, has darn near everything a teen could want. He picked out his own clothes. He could select any style he likes as long as it is within specified budget parameters. The only other restriction is that he had to wear his pants on his waist, not below his hips. He had the latest games and music. He got to stay up until ten at night. *Why did he still treat me like he hated me?* I wanted to understand where his head was.

I tried to get Tyrell to open up to me. I asked him what was wrong, and like most young kids, he vacillated between he didn't know and that nothing was wrong. I kept pressing, then he told me I was the issue. It didn't make sense to me. I asked him what I did and he had the nerve to say that I make him mad when I ask him if he's done his chores. He said that I was always on him and never gave him a chance to get it done. You can imagine my response, but I'll share. "Well child, I am the head of this house and I tell you when to get it done. You do not tell me when you are going to get to it. I gave you a time frame and told you not to get on the phone, nor watch TV, or do anything else until you have completed your chores. So, when I see you getting dressed like you are about to go outside and when I see you sitting in front of the TV, it tells me that A, you are done with your chores, or B you just did not give a darn about any of my rules."

"Momma, that's not it, he tried to tell me."

"So, what is it?" I needed to know what his issue was.

"Nothing."

"What do you mean nothing?"

"Nothing!"

"Tyrell why don't you open up?"

"I can't".

"Why not?"

"I don't know."

"Tyrell you are driving me crazy with that mess. Talk to me."

"Nothing's wrong, Mom."

"Okay fine. I'll leave it alone, but you still have to do your chores." Later that night, I discover that Tyrell had snuck out the house. He was gone until the next day. I was worried. "Tyrell, where were you."

"Nowhere."

"Oh, come on! You are kid. You had no business being out all night. Who are you running with? Are you getting high?"

"Mom, I'm tired. I am going to sleep."

"Oh no you are not! You are going to talk to me. I worried about you ever since I discovered you were gone. You know I am not well, dealing with Diabetes, why are you putting me under so much pressure?"

"I am not putting you under pressure. You are doing that to yourself."

"Little boy, I will knock you out. You do not talk to me that way". I lunged toward him. I almost wanted to hit him so hard that I'd knock some sense into this child. *How can my own flesh and blood do me like this? What an ungrateful kid.* "Tyrell, do you want to go back to your father's?"

" No, he replied.

"Well at the rate you are going, I am so ready to send you back." I yelled.

"I will never go back to him. I hate him. He doesn't love me. He only cares about himself." I could hear the pain in his voice.

"Well son, you are not giving me much choice. The only other alternative is boot camp." I was tired and needed an intervention for him. I signed Tyrell up for Boot Camp. This was actually a program run by the Los Angeles County Sheriff's department. It was a Saturday only program where volunteers from the Marine Corp discipline juveniles through a structured program that applied a militant approach. Tyrell ran away the third weekend into boot camp. The sheriff deputy told me to call him as soon as Tyrell showed up; he was sure he'd return home. He was right and when he did, I called. The deputy came with two Marines in full effect. These guys rushed through the door, grabbed Tyrell, interrogated him for not showing up at the program, then made him feel bad about putting me through so much drama. Next, they ransacked his room and made him clean it up inch by inch. They also made him scrub the floor with a toothbrush.

None of this helped. Tyrell just became more distant, and more prone to get into other non-productive things. I called my brother and asked him to take up some time with Tyrell because I believed that at this point, the kid was rebelling because of a lack of love from a father figure. More discipline was not the issue. Tyrell actually told me that he wanted to be with his uncle, but every time he called him, he was not available or has some excuse. I even called my cousin, who Tyrell enjoyed hanging around, but he was not available. I was running out of resources. I needed help with Tyrell. I was working a very demanding job at the time. I had to deal with bull crap at night, and be prepared to chair a meeting or two the very next day. My energy level had been nearly depleted from the tears, the tension, and the anger from the night before. I wanted to call in sick so many days. Sometimes, I did, but many times, I did not. You see, I was more afraid of ruining any promotional opportunities, than I was of losing my health. Somehow, I found the strength to get up and go to work as if my life was just wonderful.

The Bible says, when I am weak, he is strong. Isn't that the truth. It was in my weakest hour that I would find supernatural strength. My God had my back through all of this. Oh, there is so much more. Besides doing all I could to figure out how to help him get his act together, I was dealing with what I perceived to be racism and even a bit of favoritism on my job. I was being worked the hardest in the department. My boss demanded that I stay late, he made me feel bad when I said I had to leave to get to my family. It was a horrible situation. I darn near ran the department while he and the other two cronies were out golfing until nine in the morning, while the rest of us worked as early as six-thirty in the morning and as late as eight or nine at night (mostly me).

In my moments of struggle, I began to offer a sacrifice of praise to my God. I had been hearing my pastor speak on the topic of praising the Lord in the midst of your trials. Our victory is in the praise and worship of our Lord. Not only was I listening to what my pastor was teaching, I started reading the Bible more. I read other spiritual books and listened to tapes from my pastor's previous sermons. I needed Jesus. Here is a prayer of praise and worship that I believe helps get us through the hard times.

# In his Presence

*I bow down before you to worship you. You are an awesome God.*
*You are my refuge, my strong tower, you are my healer. You are Jehovah*
*Rapha.*
*Father, you strengthen me. How I love you and praise your name.*
*Though I physically do not feel strong enough to worship and praise you,*
*I know this praise will come out because it is the praise you desire and delight*
*in.*
*This is truly the "sacrifice of praise that you delight in"*
*You are awesome, wonderful, loving, and powerful.*

# Chapter 14

# The Relentless Warfare.

*The Weapons of our warfare are not carnal but mighty to the pulling down of strongholds. I thought I understood this scripture, but until my trials and tribulations, I had no clue of the profundity of it.*

**MJEnvision1t**

*A*ren't things supposed to get better when you pray? It seems that the more I prayed the worse things became. My own son stole my car. Around two in the morning I received a phone call that no parent wants to get.

*Hello! Is this the parent of Tyrell...?*

*Yes, this is his mother. Is he ok? What happened? I asked frantically.*

*He is ok, ma'am, but he is in custody.*

"What?" I screamed. "In custody for what?"

"Your son was caught with two other juveniles in what appeared to be a stolen vehicle.

He said it is your car, Ma'am. Do you own a black Honda Civic?" He asked.

Upset, I responded that I did own the car.

"You need to come down to the impound to get your car."

"OMG! I have to go to work in a few hours. I don't believe this. Where are you located?" He proceeded to give me the address and directions. He also let me know I could take custody of my son. That was the wrong time to tell me that. My emotional response was nothing nice.

"No, just let him stay a while. Maybe he will think about what he has done." Furiously, I hung up the phone, got out the bed and started looking for something to wear. I called one of my friends to pick me up and take me to get my car. I had no idea what condition my car would be in since the officer said my car was in a minor accident. I waited for my ride, quite impatiently. My heart was beating fast. "How could my child do this to me?" Yes, I took it personal. He did this to <u>me</u>. After all I had done for him. All the sacrifices I made for him; this is the thanks I get. My car stolen, wrecked, and a trip to the impound and police station before I had to go to work. I took that very personal. I was so upset with him.

I got my four-year old out of bed and dressed him, as well. My ride showed up, and I jumped in the car with my little boy and headed off to see what kind of trouble his big brother had gotten into. I picked up my car, it was a little scratched, and had a small dent, but nothing major, thank goodness. I did have to pay to get it out, though. It was not in my budget, but I did what I had to do. Something else was not going to get paid as a result. I stopped at the police station to talk to the arresting officer. I wanted to know what the boys were doing and what the outlook would be for my son. The officer let me know that they were driving suspiciously. "Ma'am, it was pretty obvious your son did not know how to drive, well", the officer began to explain. He went on to say, "When he or the passengers noticed us, they may have panicked, because he suddenly started driving faster, then just as quickly, he slowed down. Your son pulled over, but hit one of those short poles in the parking lot."

So, I guess that is how he damaged my car," I said with an attitude.

"I think so, ma'am". The officer replied.

"Well, unless you want to press charges, you can take your son home," the officer said.

I was so mad at my child. I really wanted to leave him in there, but my heart would not let me do it. I went ahead and signed for his release. I must have cursed the hell out of him all the way home. I was furious. *What the hell was he thinking?* I asked him after I finished raging at him. He replied like a kid who was caught with his hand in the cookie jar looking away from his accuser.

"I don't know."

"What do you mean you don't know?" I asked. "Did you not know that when you snuck in my room to take the keys that you were doing something wrong? Did you not know that since you do not have a driver's license, you could get pulled over and get cited by the police for driving without a license? Did you not know that I could have reported my car stolen and the police could have run the plates, and would have seen this was a stolen car? Do you know how bad the outcome could have been? They could have handled you as a suspect who was resisting arrest when you attempted to flee, and could have shot you? Baby boy, you better wake the hell up and look around at the world we live in. Don't nothing nice come out of run-ins with the police. You could have been beaten, or shot. You could have killed yourself or someone else if you had crashed that car. You don't know how blessed you are to just come out of this without a felony."

I had to appear in court with my son a few days later. When the DA brought up the joy ride, he also brought up a prior detainment for having a marker in his pocket when he was stopped earlier that week by the police. The stop was made for suspected graffiti. However, they did not arrest him for it, but they confiscated the marker, then let him go. I did not know about it until this hearing on the joy ride. I did not know the cops can stop your child on the streets, take their name and other identifying information, put that info into a database, let your child go, and you never know about it until something else comes up later. Is that right? Well, he was not arrested, so the defense attorney motioned to strike that information as irrelevant, and not noteworthy since there was no arrest.

My son got lucky, I mean, really blessed. He ended up being charged with driving without a license and driving without owner's permission. I did not want him to stay with me, however. I was afraid he had not learned his lesson. I asked for options. Could he go to boot camp on a farm somewhere that would show him how to be a man? How to be responsible? My son was sentenced to complete a program at a Juvenile Detention home about an hour outside of Los Angeles. It was a boy's home where there was a strict routine of chores, school, and community service. I liked the program. He could get a weekend pass to come home, but he had to earn it. My son earned his pass once, but did something stupid, so he did not earn another pass for a while. This only angered him. So, what did he do? He went AWOL from the program. Yep, showed up on my doorstep one day. My contractor, who was working on the house called me to say, uh, I think your son just came home? What? He is supposed to be in Yucaipa. What is he doing there? Please put him on the phone. What are you doing home? I asked. He replied he cannot take it there anymore. I asked how he got home. He said he caught buses. This boy was very resourceful. He was determined. He refused to let anything hold him back from what he wanted, good or bad.

I told him he had to go back or things would just get worse. He would not go. I called the program and told them he was home and asked them to come get him. The program director told me that there was nothing they could do. He breached the terms of the contract. He has proven that he does not want to do better, so they would not put any more energy into working with him. I was so hurt. The probation department put him on house arrest. *Why my child?* What did I do that was so wrong to deserve this hell? I was college educated. I owned my own home as a single woman. I worked my tail off and obtained nearly everything I had on my own. So why was this happening? Why couldn't my son see me as an example to get his life on the right track? Was he mad at me? Was he mad at his father? Was this just a bad situation that no one could be blamed for? What was driving him? I had to stay in prayer. Heck, not even prayer, just in-depth conversations with God. I asked him directly for help.

I wonder if my son mistook God's grace as a pass to go do more stupid antics. His minor juvenile activities escalated. The criminal activities increased as my son engaged deeper and deeper with the local gang. Little did I know he had joined one of the worse street gangs in LA. I was in denial. My son was a good boy. He went to a well-known Christian school. He was in private schools most of his life. He lived a couple of years with his father and was involved in sports. He did well in school. This could not be my child. No way! As my reality had it, this was my child. My child had made the decision to engage in a life-style that made him feel like a "man".

He was associating with boys and men from the streets. This made him feel like somebody. Why would anyone want that life? Why would anyone want to hang with a bunch of young men and old men who have nothing going for themselves but the street life? No job, no stability, no future. He was looking for a male role model, whether he knew it or not. He was looking to feel a part of a family of men who he looked up to. He did not have his father anymore. His father had a new wife, a new life, and that life had no room for his son. His mother worked extended hours at work. He was left to walk home from private school through gang infested territory most every day. So, what did this fourteen-year-old boy do? He joined a gang.

One day after work and school, my youngest son and I walked into our house, and when he went to play his video game, it was gone. Tyrell was not home, either. I called all of Tyrell's friends looking for him. Someone told me they thought he was on Brynhurst. That was a very rough street in L.A. It was a known drug, gang, and crack-head hang out. I hopped in my car with my little four-year-old son and I went looking for my firstborn. I took off down Crenshaw boulevard and made my way to Brynhurst. Once on that street, my heart started racing. I remembered being on that street when my oldest son was about three or four years old. It was the street where a close friend of mine lost his aunt. She was very young and pretty, but she was a drug addict. She was stopped by the police, and since she was carrying a small, but criminal amount of an illegal substance, she swallowed it when the police approached. She overdosed and died from that act. She left two small children behind. I knew what that neighborhood was about. I was hoping that was not where my son had chosen to hang out.

I drove further down the street and stopped at the next corner. I looked to my right and saw a large crowd of people wearing white T-shirts with blue Khaki pants and some with beige Khaki pants. I turned down that street and headed toward the group of gang members. I was a little nervous, but the more I thought about my son, the easier it was for me to drive right up to inquire about my son with one of the most notorious crip gangs in L.A. As I rolled through, the sea of people started stepping back to let me through, or so I thought. One guy approached my car. He looked to be in his early to mid-twenties. I rolled down my window.

"You looking for something?" he asked.

"Yeah, my son." I quickly answered with a bit of an attitude.

"Who's your son was." He asked with an authoritative voice.

"Tyrell," I replied.

He yelled to the other young folks standing around, "Any of y'all know a Tyrell?"

All I saw were heads shaking "no".

"What's his street name?"

"I don't know anything about a street name. I gave him the name Tyrell and that is the only name I know."

"Alright then momma, I got you. It's just that most of these little homies will know him by his street name."

Seconds later, someone else walked up to my car and asked, "Are you Flintstone's momma?"

I did not know anything about his street moniker at this point. I was an educated, working mother. I left that life behind me years ago. I certainly was not thinking about my son being engaged in gang life, but he was. In response to the young boy who walked up to my car, the older guy said, "Oh yeah?" It was as if it suddenly clicked with him who my son was.

"When I see that little *nigga*, I'm going to kick his [tale] all the way home. Just looking at you I can tell you don't want him around this bull."

I replied, "No, I really don't. So, if you *got to* kick his tale all the way home, then do that. I hope it wakes him up."

When I got home later, Tyrell was home. I told him I was out looking everywhere for him. He said he heard. I asked him why he took his brother's game. He said he was going to bring it back. I told him, ok, let's go get it. Then he told me he sold it. I could have choked him. I then told him to just go. So, he left. I did not hear from him for a couple of days. He went to stay with one of his knucklehead friends. My anger with him and my attempt at giving him tough love by putting him out only led to more rebellion and acting out. I grew up hearing my elders tell other parents, *"Spare the rod spoil the child, or you better whip his behind or he's going to whip you."* I never wanted to put hands on my children. I did, when the situation called for it, but I never liked doing it. In the case of Tyrell, the more discipline he received, the worse he became. He was dealing with emotional pain that neither his father or I could understand. Giving him a butt whipping, as we called it, was not the answer for Tyrell. We were angry at the choices Tyrell made and did not know how to make him change and do better. We told him he was ruing his life, but it did not phase him.

His choice impacted not only his life. His choice to join the gang meant time off work for me due to mandatory court appearances. His choices were affecting my life. They were affecting my job. I wish his dad had listened to me when I told him sending Tyrell back to me was a mistake. I worked too hard. I was not able to supervise him. Tyrell did what he wanted to do and defied my rules. I felt like he did not appreciate what I went through to take care of him. It was a slap in my face for him to choose to affiliate with gang members. I told him that if he were in jail or needed them, they couldn't help. These guys couldn't bail him out. They wouldn't send him a hygiene package when he got locked up.

I asked, "Are these really the kind of people you want to be around?"

He responded, "Mom, you don't understand. Do you think I want to do this? You don't know what I go through. I feel like one minute I want to do right and follow God and do what you want me to do. Then I feel like the devil is on my shoulder, or in my ear telling me this is me. I know you want better for me. I know you work hard. None of this has to do with you."

"Son, I love you, but you cannot live with me if this is the life you want to live. I don't want to be riding with you and someone decides they want to take you out because they are from a different gang. Both me and your brother would be at risk of being shot, along with you."

"I know mom. I don't want that to happen."

"You better decide to leave the devil's lifestyle alone and follow God. The devil is trying to destroy you. If you choose his side, you can't live here." I said with disappointment.

"So that's how you feel ma? You would put me on the streets?"

"Yes. If you don't care what happens to yourself or us, and you don't want to follow my rules, then you don't want live here."

It appeared as if my words had sunk in. He was home a little more often. He enrolled back in school, and he started going to counseling, at my insistence. I was in constant prayer that things would turn around. For the next few weeks, we spent time together as a family. We enjoyed movies together, and went shopping at the mall. On one of our outings, we even stopped to take a family portrait. Little did I know, that would be the last family picture we'd take outside of prison walls for many years to come.

Tyrell ended up in a high-speed chase with the police that ended in a car accident. I do not have the details. Honestly, I did not want to know. The accident was on the news. I called in to work letting them know I would be late and something happened with my son. I did not know the accident was on the local news until my boss asked me if my son was involved in the accident that he saw on the news? I was like, *what*? I did not see anything on the news. I could not believe this was happening to my family. I was going to spend time searching and paying for a good lawyer instead of a college for Tyrell.

The attorney that picked up my son's case was very good at her job. She never gave me all of details about the auto theft and the accident. Said it was better that I remained ignorant to it all. She quickly moved his case along and got him six months in a juvenile camp for grand theft auto, but nothing was said about the other car in the accident. It haunts me a little that I never found out what happened to the people in the other vehicle, but since the case did not turn into vehicular manslaughter, I guess that is all that matters.

I still could not stop asking, why was this happening? I served God, I loved God. I trusted God, but this was still happening. I told myself there has to be a reason. Is this for a greater testimony later? I believe that God allows us to go through certain things so that we can be used to help others. I do not think that a person who has never experienced life on the streets could be as effective in a street ministry as someone who has gone through similar struggles. I kept believing that my son's day would come when he can give his testimony to some young person on his way to make the same mistake. I kept standing and waiting on the Lord. I prayed for my son's safety as he served his time. The prayers of other saints also helped. I had a great person in my department who prayed for me and my family. My relationship with the Lord got even stronger. I was at the point where I began to claim victory for my son almost daily. I wrote words of inspiration and prayer just for his situation:

> *"My son, you are the redeemed of the Lord. You are God's chosen vessel of honor. The thief has come to steal, kill and to destroy the gift that God has placed in you. Stand Up! Rise Now! You are the redeemed of the Lord. Get back Satan! Hands off! He is not yours. He is a chosen vessel. He is covered by the blood of Jesus. It matters not how ugly the situation looks. It matters not how ugly the trials are, God is in charge.*
>
> *Son, I see you ministering to other young people; encouraging them to honor their mothers and fathers. I see you inspiring them to be all they can be.*
>
> *Father, cover my son with love, grace, and mercy.*
>
> *In Jesus' name, Amen".*

# Chapter 15

# Court again, I need me some Jesus right about now!

*Losing a child to the juvenile justice system was hard, but knowing an even bigger monster was coming for him was even worse. There was a relentless attack on my child's future, so I had to put on the whole armor of God and stand in the gap for him.*

**MJEnvisionit**

I was so happy when the lawyer took Tyrell's juvenile case and got him a short camp sentence. He was not going to lose too much of his childhood behind bars. He was supposed to be done in less than a year. I was looking forward to that. The year 2002 was going to be his year to get back on track and finish high school. I was in for a rude awakening, however. While serving time in youth authority, a new case was filed. This one was gang related. I had no idea that the local gang my son was accused of having an affiliation with was under investigation. My firstborn was going to be named as a member of this notorious criminal organization. I was shocked when he was pulled out of the juvenile system and tried as an adult under California Prop 21 that was passed in March 2000. I had no idea that two years later, my kid would be directly impacted by it.

My son and I were headed down the long road of what I call the Juvenile *Injustice* System. Tyrell had to attend juvenile court with a public defender who seemed to care, but unfortunately took ill with cancer and had to give up the case to another defender. This one was young and a bit rude. She acted as if I was asking for something unheard of when I requested my son go to a boy's camp, like those our non-melanin brothers and sisters get to send their kids. I did the research and wrote my recommendation, but it was blown off. The probation officer said that YA would be best for him. YA is Youth Authority. She said YA had the programs he needed. I do not remember everything, but at some point along the juvenile justice journey, my son's case was being evaluated for fitness to be tried as an adult.

In my estimation, the crime Tyrell was charged with had to have happened when he was fourteen years old. He was already a few months into his sentence in juvenile camp, at fifteen years old. I could not get my head around any of this. The court date came up a few months after he had been transferred from the juvenile camp to the Youth Authority. It was only two years ago; he was graduating from the eighth grade. He was living with his dad in northern California. None of us saw this coming, well at least not to this degree.

I foresaw trouble for Tyrell when his father told me was sending him back home to me. I was not prepared to receive him back. I was not able to supervise him due to my demanding schedule. I was a single mother, but he was, now, a married father. I thought he should have been responsible enough to take care of his son. He had a wife who was always on my case about what she thought I should be doing as his mother, so I felt like the two of them together were better for him. His father sent him away because, as he said, Tyrell ran away from him. That never made sense to me. He was a grown man with a military background, I do not know why he thought I could handle Tyrell better than he could. He pressed me to give him custody because he needed to be around a man, but when things got tough, I had to carry the load. In less than a year, this beautiful soul of child was chipped away and quickly becoming the hard heart of a broken teen. We found ourselves, sitting in court awaiting a verdict that would change the rest of my son's and our family's life.

I prayed so hard for him in this situation and even throughout his early childhood years. I even dedicated him to the Lord as a baby. I wondered why my son 's life was going in such a horrible direction. Was this all part of something greater? Was this leading to a purpose that he, or maybe I was called to fulfill? My faith was certainly being tested by this time. I refused to quit on my child. I did not want to see my son get eaten alive by a justice system that was not designed to correct or rehabilitate men of color. I searched for organizations that could help me understand how to navigate the juvenile justice system, and even more importantly, understand how this whole *juvenile tried as an adult* thing was going to play out. I wanted to stop the minions from hauling my son away like he was a criminal. I never accepted that stigma for him. I saw a beautiful, loving, respectful little boy behind the pain. I needed to rescue him. I got involved with the Youth Justice Coalition (YJC) and the Ella Baker Center for Human Rights.

These organizations provided a safe space for parents of incarcerated youth to talk about the pain, help bring solutions, and stand for justice. The focus was on education in the juvenile system and stopping use of the gang database. It was being used by the police department to officially associate youth with gangs. The bad part was that an officer could inaccurately define your child as a gang member or affiliate him. The office would use meaningless criteria such as seeing a kid with a known gang member, so the kid must have been affiliated with the gang. I remember sitting at the table in Downtown Los Angeles with members of the YJC and Civil Rights Watch talking to the LA County Department of Probation leaders and a newly appointed (at that time) gang Czar about our concerns as parents and citizens. We let these people know that not every child is a gang member who lives in a black or brown community and just because his or her brother or sister is in a gang, that does not mean the other sibling is. This was dear to me because my son was about to be tried as an adult due to his gang affiliation. Never mind that he did not have any significant priors. Never mind that he had just graduated from 8th grade as an honor roll student. They did not care that my son had two parents who loved him enough to pay for private school and provided a roof over his head. He did not come from drug users, nor a family with a history of gang affiliation, yet, he was treated as if he was the very leader himself. Unfortunately, this was a time in

California's history where politicians were pushing a crime bill that would demonstrate they were getting on tough on crime. The sad truth that was and still is well known in communities of color is that getting tough on crime only means getting tough on black and brown males.

The dreadful day arrived in 2003, our family was altogether sitting in the court room to hear a case being brought against my son. My mom and I attended the earlier hearings in juvenile court, but now, he was being tried as an adult in the criminal court system. As I sat in the court room listening to the charges and allegations, I felt like I was in a bad movie. *Why were we here? Why was he being tried as an adult? He had not shot, stabbed, or killed anyone. Why was he being treated so harshly?* Allegations of a planned robbery, a brandished weapon, and all scoped out while we were out shopping for shoes. Camera footage was pulled in from nearby stores to help identify the suspects. I was shocked when the shoe store worker said my son came in with me and his little brother the day before the crime. The DA tried to paint a picture that my son had pre-planned a robbery. The judge questioned the DA about why he was going so hard on Tyrell, especially since he did not have a criminal record. The DA argued some precedent case to justify his position, and ultimately won his case. When the verdict was rendered, the judge shared a short story about himself as a kid and that he made stupid mistakes, but someone gave him a chance to do better. Afterward, he suggested that Tyrell sign up for fire camp once he was checked in at intake. He made it sound so simple. Little did he know and little did we know that my son would never be allowed to sign up for fire camp because the department of corrections categorized him as a level 4 criminal. No fire camp for him. He was tried as an adult and treated as a career criminal.

My son was going to do hard time. I never accepted it. I kept praying and believing God for his release. I put my house up for a lawyer. I paid a lot of money only to see my son in handcuffs and off to serve time with grown men. *What was God up to? Why was he allowing this for my son?* As I asked this question, it came to me that my son's life was going to be a testimony for someone else. God allowed it like he allowed Job to go through pure hell. He allowed Job to be tested. My son was crying out to me and to his father all along. His was a voice in the distance that I kept hearing in the background of my life and in the forefront. In the background, as I journeyed from welfare to work…. I worked very hard to make sure my kids did not have to want for anything. Unfortunately, I found myself struggling a lot. I had a roof over my head. I had nice cars throughout my life, I even owned my own home. It was in the neighborhood of the first house that I brought that my eldest son got introduced to the gang life. I was oblivious though. I was working so hard to pay for his private school and to pay my way through school, that I never noticed. I was a single mom of two when my eldest got caught up. It happened so quickly after that phone call from his dad. The one saying, "hey Monique", I am sending Tyrell back home to you.

I was working in corporate America. I was going back to school for my masters soon after I had gotten my second son potty trained. I was going to prove to myself that being a single mom was not going to stop me from achieving success in life. I kept pushing. I thought it was going to be all good when I let him go live with his dad. I was proud of the young man was becoming. Smart, handsome, respectful. He was living with a father who had been in the military who was a business owner, and who was married. The perfect role model for our male child. I expected he was going to UCLA. He said he would. I was going to obtain my MBA with a Juris Doctorate in Business Law. I had been accepted to Pepperdine's graduate school. All so promising, but our plans were not going to be realized. Our plans are not always God's plans.

***

I was strong-willed and confident in my own abilities that I did not think I needed a man to help me raise my sons, especially if they did not want to be involved. I felt like I just needed to keep them in good schools and covered in prayer.

That is not the way things turned out. Ultimately, I made it from welfare to a six-figures and to home ownership in a nicer community. The journey was not smooth. I became a workaholic. Working and achieving became drugs for me. It became my addiction to get over the hurt and pain of losing my son to the system. I worked harder and harder than ever. Not just in my work career, but in youth activism, and in obtaining higher learning. I had been working so hard early on that my son's voice was merely a voice in the distance, but after our experience with the juvenile justice system, I worked harder, but with his voice in the forefront now.

God was in the background making a way for my peace to manifest. Little by little, I became stronger and stronger with each and very trial. I kept praying and praising the Lord no matter how bad things looked. I thank God Tyrell had my mom and I to support him through it all. So many young men who join gangs really do live and die for the gang. They have a loyalty that those of us who are not involved could never understand. One way I can express how this time felt to me, and possibly to my son, is in a poem I wrote at the end of this chapter. I hope it speaks to you and helps put a light on what some of our young men go through when there is no balance in the lives of working parents, and no good male role model in the home.

### Reflection

*Did you realize that working long hours could be a drug for someone? Staying super busy keeps the mind occupied to the point it cannot give attention to anything else. This becomes a way to drown out undesirable thoughts about unfavorable situations. Becoming a workaholic is how some hide their pain.*

# Young Black King

*I wish I could have protected you from that horrific sting*
*The streets targeted you as its prey*
*The gang was out there watching you as you went about your day*
*Soon they'd realize you were a kid on his own*
*Mom was working and could not pick you up and keep you out of the danger zone*
*It was time to make you feel welcome in your neighborhood*
*The streets were calling you to come rep the hood*
*That is the story of a young black king, held back from his crown*
*A casualty of the working family with no village to hold them down*
*Mom and a dad were always busy and rarely around.*
*They didn't realize the predators were awaiting*
*The right moment to lure you, they were contemplating*
*When they'd find this innocent child unsupervised*
*They'd tempt him with a false sense of family, sell him lies*
*Oh and a few pieces of gold, that would sure get him sold*
*On what they had to offer that could bring him into their fold.*
*While mama worked to keep a roof over her children's head*
*Making sure her babies would never go unfed*
*She kept climbing the corporate ladder*
*Daddy had his freedom, he lived in his own kingdom*
*He thought just sending a check was all that really mattered*
*Mom and Dad missed it, that was not the stuff he needed;*
*Not the toys, good school, clothes or food, even though he received it*
*Neither of you could protect this little king from being swallowed up by the streets*
*The streets that gave him a sense of family*
*The streets that gave him a sense of pride*
*The streets that took him on a little joyride*
*The streets that lead him into confinement*
*Because he never received his dad's refinement*
*While locked away amongst prisoners and guards*
*He found out that life was really hard*
*The fast money stopped, no package from the homey*
*The one he thought was family*
*He'd soon be thankful to his mom and nana for taking action*
*The "Queens Who Love Me" should be his social media caption*

# Chapter 16

# Hey Girl, You're Resilient

*The battle is in the mind, but fatigue is felt in our bodies when we have endured worry and strife far too long. I am thankful for the scripture that uplifts me when I am worn: But they who wait upon the Lord shall renew their strength; they shall mount up with wings like eagles; they shall run and not be weary; they shall walk and not faint. Isaiah 40:31 KJV*

MJEnvisionit

I had to pick up the pieces from the aftermath of my firstborn son's ordeal. I stood on the promises of God, I prayed and I even shed tears every now and then. The battle was rough. We both lost custody of our son, his father and I. We lost him to the criminal justice system, via a machine known as the PIC. *The PIC was and is the Prison Industrial Complex. It's been around since 1973, but it was in 1997 that the term PIC was coined by Angela Davis, an activist and scholar who gave a speech that became an essay about the pipeline to prison that young black and brown men were becoming the most targeted. The prison industry was privatized and the number of arrests of black and brown young men sky rocketed.* [2]

This move to privatize prisons had massive negative impact on black and brown youth. They were being sucked into this machine by the droves. It hurt to see this happen to my own son. Especially when I purposely put in effort to keep this from happening. I was hurt to my core. I cried many days. Eventually, I became closer to the Creator of the Universe, God. Through every problem I faced, I got stronger. I do not know about his father, but for me, I was able to move forward in peace. A peace that I cannot explain. It did not come on me immediately after the verdict. It took some time. Little by little, I started making small changes in my life, starting with learning to tell my supervisor, no I cannot work late this time. I had another son to focus my attention on and I did not want him to experience anything his brother went through. My mindset shifted to becoming stronger and supportive of my son while he served his time. He was going to be housed in a separate dorm away from the male adults, because he was under 18. He would be transferred into general population once he became of age. For now, I was focused on praying him through. I asked God to bring him home sooner than what the courts had ordered. I moved in faith that God would answer my prayers. It was 2003 and my baby boy was six years old. Both he and I had a lot more life to live.

I started to enjoy life. I joined the water club with employees at my job. The club would take trips to lakes in California, a river in Laughlin, Nevada and a beautiful lake and resort in Lake Havasu, Arizona. I did not have time to be working late everyday (at least not as much). I was ready to start enjoying the weekends. I picked up a new sport after joining the club. *Time to go Jet skiing!* I came to really enjoy riding on the choppy waves of the local lakes. The breeze in my face was rejuvenating. The ability to go as fast as I wanted and show out a bit with my friends was exhilarating! I enjoyed it so much that I bought a time share on Lake Havasu in the resort area. This was a few months after Tyrell's sentence. I would not only go out with the water club, but with my time share, I could bring others. Life was getting better. I also started focusing more on Jamar. He was almost seven now. Time to start focusing on this child's talents and helping him to develop them. *Jamar can play some basketball!* This kid could handle a ball at the age of two and a half. He was going to be an NBA star if I had anything to do with it. This boy is so cute, so funny, and can dance. He does not take life seriously, though, but why not, he is just a kid. I wish I had his nonchalant attitude about life early on. It would have saved me some stress. I guess I would not have appreciated how far I had come if I had not experienced so much adversity.

During one of my outings with Jamar, I ran into an old boyfriend. We lost contact after he had been busted for fraud when Tyrell was very young. In Vernon's mind, he was only doing business like any other entrepreneur. He hired a lawyer to fight for him, but he lost the case. This man was so business savvy and always knew how to get money when he needed it. He maintained his connections, so when he finished serving his time, he came out ready to get back to it. He immediately started up another business, put solid employees in place, and was back on top. Wow! How intriguing. To me, this brother had it going on. Nothing would hold him down. No excuses! It is no wonder why I was impressed. I am a go getter myself. I do not let bad breaks, or circumstances stop me from reaching my goals. I hate excuses. They are just the lazy person's justification for not going after success.

As my baby boy and I were leaving the movie theater and walking to our car parked underground at the very popular Howard Hughes Center in West Los Angeles, we heard someone yell out to me from a black Mercedes E320 trying to get my attention. I was so surprised to see that it was a blast from my past.

"Vernon! Oh my God!!!" *Vernon told the lady in his passenger seat, to wait a moment, then got out of the car and gave me the tightest and longest hug, ever.* Anyone who saw us could immediately tell that we had some sort of connection and missed each other dearly. I wonder what she was thinking while watching our interaction? Vernon was all smiles.

"Nikki, it is so nice to see you again. Wow! You look good. What have you been doing all this time?"

"Well, just working and taking care of my kids, what about you? What have you been doing all this time?"

"I have been making money, you know me. I am self-employed, so I stay on the grind, but I can say I do make time for fun. Why don't you give me your number so we can catch up?"

We exchanged numbers and later that evening, Vernon called me and invited me out to dinner for later in the week. I said yes. We met up the following Friday for dinner and from there we went dancing. I had a nice time with him. We reminisced about the past, all the way back to our flirtatious high school days and to the turbulent times we had before he was arrested. All in all, we had good memories. We went out a few more times, before he started traveling again. The traveling brought some tension, but we eventually worked through them. I don't know if I just tolerated it because of the material things he had and shared with me, or if it was true love, or simply the excitement. Vernon and I had chances in the past to be a good couple, but they never came to full fruition. The first time was when I was fourteen and he was 18. I shared previously how I had such a crush on him until he told me he was getting married. Another time was when Tyrell was about two or three years old. It was close to the time I met AK and Reggie. Vernon and I dated for a little while when I lived in the apartment where most of my time was spent in a love triangle with Reggie. I dated Vernon for a short while, just before getting entangled with Alex, and later Reggie. Vernon's fraud case came up at that time and ultimately the relationship.

Here we are again. Vernon, the man I crushed on in high school was back. After a few more dates, Vernon was talking marriage. It sounded good. But was it too late? I was just getting to know a very nice man who had an amazing singing voice. I really liked him. I had been having fun with him and enjoying his lifestyle: family events, karaoke, line dancing, *and he could dance!* This guy was real. I was not used to a man like him. He didn't have a lot of money. He didn't drive a fancy car, but he was saving to buy a home and was trying to launch his singing career. He was very humble. He took great care of his sons. He was a well-rounded guy, but he was not clear about his feelings toward me. He would not let me all the way in to his heart. I was not sure if I wanted to let him go to pursue a relationship with Vernon, or if I should give him more time. I didn't want to wait too long and miss an opportunity to be married to someone who I believed could be a good provider and that I knew loved me. There would be no guess work with Vernon, although my heart was feeling the new guy. Finally, I could no longer see the new guy. Vernon was getting very serious. The new guy was not showing me that he wanted me as much as Vernon did. I asked him how he felt and his response was that he liked me. There was no depth, however. I finally told him that things were getting serious and Vernon wanted to marry me. My heart was a little broken when he did not try to stop me. At this point, I was no longer seeing Reggie. If he were around, I probably would have let him stop me. I moved forward with Vernon.

***

'At *Laaassst*!'

Etta James played as I walked down the aisle. serene water glistened; floating candles gave us a shimmering light. The audience was in awe of my beauty. The ceiling opened up, and doves ascended to the sky. What a scene. What a memorable moment.

Do you…. "I Do."

Do you…. "I Do."

You may kiss the bride! *Done*. We did it!

Off to the honeymoon. I was excited. I could not believe I was married and on my way to enjoy my husband for a week at a gorgeous lakeside resort in Nevada. This place was so nice. I loved the marble entry way. *How lovely*. I felt like I was on top of the world. The hard times I experienced as a single mom, was all over now. I was being rewarded for all of suffering. *Thank you, Lord! You saw my pain and you are blessing me in deed*. "Hey babe", Vernon called to me as he walked over to the kitchenette in our honeymoon suite to grab an apple. Do you want to go out on the water tomorrow? We can rent a boat and tour the lake after breakfast." That sounded good to me. I loved being on the water and so did Vernon. He was once featured in a magazine article for his close win in a jet ski contest from Long Beach, CA to Catalina. Tomorrow was going to be so much fun, but today we were just going to relax, take a stroll, have a nice dinner, then enjoy each other as husband and wife in this luxurious hotel nestled in Lake Los Vegas, a hidden treasure of Nevada.

"Good morning, sweet heart", he said in a loving tone while looking into my eyes.

"Good morning! I can't believe we are married now."

"Me either," Vernon replied, I finally got my Nikki."

"Do you remember that day at the bus stop?" I asked, "you were eighteen years old. I was going on fifteen. You had just gotten off from work at Taco Bell. You were still wearing your uniform. I was walking by with a couple of my friends. You stopped me and said 'you needed to tell me something.' I told them to go on and I would catch up later. You let me know that you really liked me, but I was too young for you. I was crushing on you so hard back then."

Vernon laughed as I continued reminiscing, "I used to go up to Taco Bell after school with my friends just to see you. I thought you were so cute. That smile, oh my God! I would blush whenever you smiled at me. You and I would talk all the time. We eventually started hanging out together."

""I remember having you come visit me at my mom's house. You met my sister." Vernon replied.

"Uh huh, I had caught the bus after school. I had no business over there with you. My mom would have beat my tale.", I said laughing.

"I had always hoped we would be together one day. You were a gentleman. You let me down easy when you told me our age difference was not working for us. I went on with my life, and it turns out, you had actually gotten married shortly after to your high school sweetheart."

Vernon nodded his head, "Yes, I remember. I really did care about you and I did not want to hurt you. I did realize you were jail bait, so I had to just move on, but we are together now. Let's get dressed and get some breakfast. I can't wait to get you out on the water."

The day was sunny, with a light breeze. It was indeed a nice day to be out on the water. It was totally relaxing. We got along well during the entire time, no arguments about petty things. There was something that many did not know about us. We had begun arguing more often than we should have so early in this restart of a relationship. The night of the wedding rehearsal, we had a disagreement. I wanted to call the wedding off out of emotions, but I realized that it was just that, emotions. The time we spent on our honeymoon made me glad that I went forward with it. Vernon showed me how to steer a boat. This was something new for me. I was good at jet skiing, but I had never steered a boat. I grew up riding in them with my grandfather, but that was it. I was excited to learn something new. I know that is why I was intrigued by Vernon. He was willing to do things that the guys I was used to being around, were not. The time we spent together was precious. I did not want to leave the beautiful resort, but reality was setting in and it was time to pack up and head home.

We had been home about two weeks and it was back to the busy work life. I knew what was coming when Vernon said there was a real estate seminar in Arizona he was looking into. Looking into meant he was going. We had just returned from our honeymoon and he was off and running. I was okay with him going out of town for business, but it seemed as if he was always taking off. While he was away promoting his business, I began to get sick. I knew what I was feeling, but I wanted to be sure, so I took a pregnancy test. The little pink line appeared and it was confirmed, I was having another baby. I must have been pregnant when I walked down the aisle because I was already nine weeks and we had been back from the honeymoon about four weeks. I was thirty-six years old and by the time my new bundle of joy would be born, I would have turned thirty-seven.

The timing of this baby was eight years after having Jamar and eighteen years after Tyrell. I had a huge age gap between my children because each time I gave birth, I told myself I was done. My position was that I would only have another baby if I got married. I did pretty good until I met Jamar's father. The third one was the charm though. I was having this baby with my husband. He was my high school crush and now I was his wife and we were having a baby. He was excited. The further along I was in the pregnancy, the more Vernon began to stay closer to home. He did not want to miss the birth of his child. At this point we were living in my apartment in West Los Angles. My dad was the owner. We were in a nice school district and a desirable part of town. I loved where we were in terms of location, but I was not happy about the size of our living quarters. Also, my dad did not want to invest money upgrading the exterior. We needed to move.

A few weeks before my good news broke about the baby, Vernon and I got a call from his auntie telling him to come out to Palmdale to look at a new home community they were building in the Antelope Valley area. We took the one-hour drive and fell in love with the homes. We put an offer in and awaited the build. The house would be ready a few months after the baby was estimated to be born. She was due in December 2005. We would be moving into the new house around March 2006. I could not wait to get that house and start decorating the baby's room, as well as looking for furniture. That was a ways off. At this point we were simply planning for a baby bed and only that which was necessary for a two-bedroom apartment.

My water broke a couple of weeks early. It is no wonder because I was doing a lot. I had gotten my real estate license and was selling houses while working fulltime for a successful auto parts manufacturer. I was getting ready for bed. I had just come out of the bathroom after taking my shower when I walked toward my bedroom and felt a rush of water run down my legs. I yelled out that my water broke. Vernon picked me up and carried me down stairs to his car with Jamar, and my play daughter in tow. My play daughter was a young lady who moved in with me after having issues at home. She took to me and I to her. She was a sweetheart, and she was Tyrell's ex-girlfriend. She grabbed my travel bag and Jamar's hand. They followed Vernon quickly to the car. We headed to Torrance Memorial, I had already pre-registered, so there would be no delays getting admitted. It was November 16, 2005, and a few hours later, we were welcoming our little girl! Kalani into the world. She was a beautiful 9lb baby who looked just like her daddy and her grandmother. Her daddy was so excited to cut her umbilical cord. Not only were we proud parents of a newborn, we were also the proud owners of a 3200 square foot home in Palmdale, California that was being built.

Shortly after I gave birth, I started suffering with sever back pain. I could not sit for long periods. Physical therapy helped a little, but sitting at the computer all day took its toll. I took time off work, that extended to a full year. During this time, I began writing a book and writing plays. I also created an after-school program for teens. I did all of this from my laptop, mostly sitting on the couch or working from my bed, or even the kitchen table. I never did know how to shut my brain off. Vernon loved this about me and would help me as much as he could when he was home. He helped me establish the afterschool program as a 501c3 non-profit organization. I named it Golden Steps Youth and Families.

I became more active with my non-profit once our baby girl had turned six or seven months. I planned an event to bring awareness about the prison industrial complex (PIC). Tyrell was my motivation for establishing the non-profit organization that was focused on steering, what was popularly called, at-risk youth away from trouble, and toward activities that allowed them to demonstrate, and even discover their talents. I knew from what my son went through, that kids needed something to keep their minds occupied. Vernon seemed to understand the vision. He was the reason I was able to start up the 501c3. He helped me establish a board of directors, do fundraising, and promote it. The non-profit used performing arts to engage youth and the community. It was focused on youth between the ages of 14 to 18. They were my inspiration for writing plays that depicted social justice issues, the epidemic of incarceration among black and brown male youth, and the rise of street fighting among black and brown teen boys and girls. I wrote plays and short skits that featured the work of the Ella Baker Center for Human Rights to push for books, not bars for youth in our society. Education, vocation, and behavior management were impressed upon the teens through dramatic performances. All was made possible through participation by youth in my community, collaboration with their high schools and support from the Youth Justice Coalition. And the Ella Baker Center.

Another goal of my non-profit was to bring awareness about new bills being presented that could hurt or help our youth. I was glad I made a connection with the organizations that were fighting for justice. I traveled to Sacramento, California with these groups to protest the injustices happening in the juvenile justice system. Spreading awareness was important to me because I did not want my son's incarceration to be in vain. The non-profit brought in kids from the community and interested groups. Various organizations and showed interest, such as art centers, a philanthropist from Washington DC, the local Economic Development Department, and a couple of churches inquired with me about leading their youth department. The love for what I was doing flattered me, but it did not pay the bills. I started from my three-car garage and the main office inside the 3200 sqft house Vernon and I lived in.

Eventually we were sponsored by an arts organization and were able to hold dance classes, as well as have an office at the Cedar Center in Lancaster, California. The City of Palmdale invited my organization to hold an afterschool program at a neighborhood house funded by grants and constructed by a popular vocation and education program called Youth Build. It was at the neighborhood house where we held a book drive, had a couple of seasonal events, and helped kids in the neighborhood with homework and reading. I was no longer working out of our house which turned out to be a good thing because we would soon lose it to foreclosure. I thought the large beautiful home we purchased, or rather, I purchased in my name, was going to be our family home. I was wrong.

Vernon was an entrepreneur, real estate investor, and had money making on his mind, all the time. I was looking for a place for our family to be planted and he was looking for a flip. The risk he took to flip the property was all on me. Of course, this is what led to the downfall of our marriage. Vernon and I began to argue about finances and his constant leaving. The arguing became more and more intense. I was angry for many reasons. I should never have gotten married to him. He was the same guy that was always leaving me to go out of town. He was the same man that I thought was a "nerd" and turned out to be a con artist. I knew better, so what was I thinking to get into a relationship with him for the third time? We argued the night of our wedding rehearsal. I wanted to call it off, then, but I was so vested. I went forward. Vernon was a man who loved his children. He made sure they had what they needed. I know this because I observed how he provided for them. I knew he would I stayed with him hoping for the best and because we now had a daughter, I wanted to be sure she experienced living life with her daddy. I loved seeing him interact with her. He looked at her with love in his eyes, and was always smiling when he was with her. I did not have to worry about him being a good father. I knew he was capable. I would ask him to watch her and he would do it, even if he had something else going. I remember a time when he was about to leave town, but I was unaware until I asked for his help.

"Vernon, I need you to watch Kalani so I can focus on the event." I told him.

"Ok babe, I will take her with me." He responded without hesitation.

"Oh! Where are you going?" I didn't know he was leaving, again.

"I have to do a seminar."

"So, who will watch her?"

"My sister."

"I will just keep her with me. I am not comfortable with you just taking her only to drop her off."

He responded by telling me that she would be in good hands. That he was just going to drop her off while he did the seminar and pick her up after. I gave in, but not happily.

I heard when Vernon said he had a business opportunity, but deep inside, I really heard, *he was leaving again.* He just could not stay home. I will give him credit for taking responsibility for our daughter; for loving her and making sure she had everything she needed. I was thankful that he helped me with the big event for Golden Steps. The nonprofit took a lot of time. I did not have a large volunteer base. I didn't have enough funding from grants to pay myself an income. I used most of my own money. Vernon's ability to promote events, motivate people into making decisions, and his all-around business savvy, motivated me to push and build the foundation. I owe what I have learned as an entrepreneur from Vernon. He was open to testing new markets and trying something different. I move that way, myself. I am not afraid to try a new business idea, or put a book out about my life. I started this book when he and I found out I was pregnant with our daughter. It should have worked out between us, but it did not.

Unfortunately, his life was full of secrets. He could not be 100% transparent with me about what was going on financially. I found myself taking on the full mortgage after he said he had it covered. I was not able to make enough money to pay myself from the proceeds of Golden Steps. I asked him over and over again what his plan was for the house, for our financial well-being. He said a lot but said nothing. I was no longer working because of the toll the last pregnancy took on my back. I had an injury that was reignited with the pregnancy weight gain. I could hardly move around. I was on disability from my job. I still brought in just enough to cover the $3000 a month mortgage, but everything else began to suffer. I was also losing the house I had rented out in Los Angeles.

I realized later that he never intended to stay in that house. He wanted to flip it. He kept trying to get me to agree to bring an investor in to help us out, but I did not understand how that would help. He never explained it, either. My trust in him began to dwindle to nothing. I saw red flags before we got married, but ignored them. He could not be honest with people that invested in his business ventures, not even my parents. Not even his so-called boys. He was not transparent. He made excuses when things went bad in business saying, basically, it's just a risk people take. *No*, that was not what I wanted to hear. That was not what my parents, who were on a fixed income, needed to hear. He looked at everything transactionally. He treated our family like a business deal. We were not a business. We were his family, or so I thought. I guess to him, we were an opportunity.

I should have expected this because of the way he did business. He did not seem to care if folks put in their life savings because they trusted the opportunity he presented. He was so savvy in working with other people's money that it became a game of "I bet I can get the money." The sad part is that he did not feel the hit because all risk was on others. He cared about who he cared about. He loved who he loved, he had a sweet demeanor and loved his children, but I believe he was detached. He would play gospel music all the time, but would still do shady things. I was struggling with trusting him. He seemed legit on the one hand, but suspect on the other. I'd talk to him about what he was doing and why I thought it was wrong. I suggested he go to God about his approach, but he did not see it the same way. I observed the way he moved, so I should have known that something wasn't right.

I wonder how many people move forward in a relationship, hoping it will work out because the person is attractive to them, or has material things that others covet? Women please be careful of the man you set your sights on. Do not get caught up in looks or the "stuff". The fancy cars, nice outfit, or sexy smile might be a ploy to get you. Those brothers have plenty of women who want the same thing as you. Please do not be blind! Unless that man is a rare jewel, a man of God, I mean a true man of God, he will not be held responsible for the hell he will take you through. Have you heard the song, *It ain't my fault*? That will be his theme song whenever you get your feelings hurt and want him to be accountable, or sorry for hurting you. I am talking from experience. My experiences with men shaped the strong woman I am today. I had to go through hell first. My way of thinking about life and my place in it helped me in one way, but hurt me in others. You see, I felt like I could help a guy to become better. I could bring him to the Lord. I could push him to improve. I could help him leave the street life. Some might call what I was doing, missionary dating. I wanted to change that, so I got with Vernon. I thought he was going to elevate me. I looked at appearances. I did not take time to dig deeper. I could have kept myself from a lot of disappointment if I had. I can tell you; I learned a lot while going through hell. I hope I can help prevent others from going through the same.

## Reflection

*Have you wondered if God was trying to show you something in a situation? Have you ever stopped to think what it is that you may be doing to attract a certain "type"? It is life changing when you can stop and reflect on your experiences and realize the role you played, and change it going forward.*

# Chapter 17

# Resilience After the Battle:

*Resilient people are like gold that is purified through the fire. It becomes a high-value commodity, as do we. Our Resilience is needed in the earth. It is a high-value commodity that will make a difference in the lives of others.*

MJEnvisionit

I filed for divorce from Vernon after almost three years of marriage. While going through the divorce, I had to figure out how to keep my house in Los Angeles and in the Antelope Valley. My tenant was playing games with the rent for the Los Angeles house. I was so busy trying to save the new house that I could not keep up the mortgage on the first house. I had to give up the Youth Foundation and get back to work where I could receive a regular paycheck. I did not want to make that decision. I tried to get into teaching so that I could continue working with kids. I got my emergency teaching credential and started substitute teaching for three school districts. This did not pay enough. In order to make the kind of money I had gotten used to, I would have to become an administrator, such as a principal or superintendent, maybe even a counselor. I was not fully convinced that education was the right path, but I hung in there with it and also got my house in the Antelope Valley certified as a foster family home. I loved kids, so I figured fostering would be fulfilling and help me stay above water, financially.

I got into this situation because I trusted that my husband was going to take care of us. I was not used to trusting anyone but myself. I tried to do something different and that was to trust someone else. Since we moved so far away, my workman's comp ran out, and I had filed for permanent disability, I needed to cash out my 401K and roll it over into an IRA. I talked to my husband about not going back to work with the auto manufacturer, but instead work with him to build up his business and develop my non-profit. He said he could take care of us. So, I terminated my employment when the company-paid disability ran out and applied for permanent disability. I had no idea this would be such a long process. As I went through the disability process, my marriage was going through its own process of falling apart. We were headed for divorce. Vernon did not pay the mortgage; he was scrambling to find the money. He would tell me he was working with an investor, but nothing panned out. We fought about the house. I was angry with him almost all of the time, so we eventually divorced.

Even though I started foster care and teaching, all after the divorce, I could not maintain. I was losing my two properties because it had been too long before I could generate enough income. I ended up doing a short sale on the house in the Antelope Valley, but I lost the house in Los Angeles. I had to apply for short term government assistance. I got on the food stamp program. The foster care and substitute teacher's income had not picked up quickly enough. I had to figure out my next move. I began to set new goals. I wrote down the amount of money I envisioned for my family to not only survive, but to thrive! I began claiming a six-figure income for myself. I knew it had to start somewhere. I looked into jobs that paid more than the average and researched the skills required. I spent time on the internet and in books getting myself updated on the latest software.

As I continued my search, I saw there were growing opportunities in the Aerospace industry for something called Earned Value Management. I researched that, too. I called my aunt who worked in the industry and asked her about it. She gave me a little background then directed me to a website to learn more. I put myself in position for an opportunity. I was ready! I was called for an interview after I applied for a job with one of the largest aerospace and defense companies in the world. I was excited to see my life changing for the better. I realized that in order for me to achieve my goals, I needed to put into practice what I had learned in the scriptures. I had to write the vision and make it plain as recorded in Habakkuk 2:2 KJV. The vision I had for my life was tarrying; it was taking too long in my eyes. It was time to write it down. I had goals, but they were in my head. Once I wrote down my vision concerning how much I needed to make in earnings, I began to see it manifest. Doors were beginning to open in places I had tried in the past, but could not even get a foot in. I knew that in order to live, not just survive, I had to make more money.

I was in my mid-twenties when I began earning over forty-five thousand annually. By the time I got my first house, at twenty-nine, I was making just under sixty-thousand. That salary increased a little more by the time my husband and I got married. It was ok since my husband and I could split expenses. That situation ended, so I had to find a way to make more on my next job. I lived in California where the cost of living was high. I had a large student loan to pay each month. I wrote down how much I wanted to make, at minimum. I got more than I was looking for when I was hired on with a major aerospace company. My financial situation was on its way to recovery. Writing the vision and making it plain, believing I could, and taking action helped me overcome the resistance I had been facing in my financial journey!

I experienced resilience in my financial position and in other areas. Resilience in my relationships was also shining through. I think back to my past dealings with men and I see where I have overcome hard situations. I was the other woman, the side chick, or the number one. There were times when I was the only woman that the man wanted in his life, but, unfortunately, I did not want him. I bore children by two different men who were not ready to commit to me. I later gave birth to a third child for a man who made me his wife. I also bore the responsibilities and consequences that came with those decisions. I wonder what direction my life would have gone in if I had waited and allowed God to choose for me? What if I had known how to listen to God back then, or rather to his Holy Spirit? Would I have waited for God's man to find me? Maybe the direction and path that my children's lives have taken would have been different.

Those are all "what ifs". Although it is common for us to ponder different scenarios, we know we cannot go back and change the past. We have to accept what has happened, learn from it, and apply lessons as you move on. My life happened the way it happened and my children went through what they went through. I pray it was for a purpose. I hope it was for you, the person reading this book today. I hope and pray it was for the person who will one day meet my sons and my daughter and listen to their story; how they struggled and overcame!

Our battles in life seem to never end. I will tell you battles come and go. It is up to us to decide to be victorious and live to win the next battle. Life teaches us great lessons. If we are wise enough to learn from them, and not play the victim, we can overcome quicker and be stronger for the next event. Life is relentless. It keeps on going. As long as we have breath, we will keep living through some stuff. How we do it is the key. Do we do it bowed down with heavy hearts, living a life of regret, tears, playing the victim all the time? Defeated? Broken? Bitter? Some might say, yes. *At least that is how they are living.* I wonder if they would stop taking on an attitude of defeat if they could step outside of themselves, and look from above at the way they are behaving, thinking, and being? Would they stop? If you could see that you have a choice to live in joy and be at peace with yourself and others, would you make the mindset shift to do it?

Often times, people get buried in their anger, their disappointment, and their desire to have what others have acquired, and they cannot see how to do better. I have been through losses; material and relational. I have experienced hurt by men, as well as co-workers who smiled in my face, but threw me under the bus or stabbed me in the back. I did not allow myself to stay in my place of pain. I took the hits as if I were in a boxing ring. I may have leaned on the ropes to catch my breath, but after, I pulled myself together through the power of prayer and praise to my Heavenly Father. I have been able to draw back my spiritual fist to take that spiritual punch, and with the power and authority of the name of Jesus, Yeshua Hamashiach, and hit the enemy of my destiny with a blow that is infused with dynamite to scatter him and his imps away. This is the power of the living God and this is how I fight my battles.

If I had not understood what it meant to fight our battles through God, I do not think I could have handled my son being locked up at such a young age. If I did not know how to stand in the proverbial gap to fight for him from a spiritual perspective, I wonder if he would have survived prison the way he did. There were moments I was so scared for him, but I would get into my prayer position and call on God. I know my Lord heard me. There were angels inside the prison keeping watch when he had come down with pneumonia. No one from the prison called me. My son was in the hospital fighting to beat this virus and I would not have known anything if it were not for my family and the people they knew. A man who was a close family friend of my beloved aunt who has since passed on to glory, reached out to her in order to get a message to me. He said inmates were asking where my son was since no one had seen him after he was taken away from his cell by medics. The man looked into it and found out my son's condition. He immediately told my aunt, and she called to let me know he was in the hospital ward with pneumonia right away.

I called up to that prison and I made sure they knew Tyrell had a mother who cared and people who knew what the deal was. They didn't know who let us know, I kept that under wraps, but they knew we had a way of finding out. I tried to use clout and impressive terms to ensure they understood the stock Tyrell came from. I threatened to get a lawyer to help me ensure my son was getting good care. I called every other day and asked for a status. I got it, too. There were other times when my son was unfairly beaten by officers. They rushed his cell and when he resisted, they went in on him. *First, how are you going to rush into a cell when someone was sleeping and had to be awaken to that? Who wouldn't immediately try to protect themselves?* Anyway, I wrote a letter to the warden concerning the treatment. I also wrote a letter about the pneumonia case and not notifying me, his mother. I wrote a letter when my son was no longer receiving his packages with hygiene and stationery. I wrote a letter when the state department of corrections tried to give him another case for protecting himself after someone tried to attack him. I was always fighting for my son, in the physical and spiritual realm. I could not wait for him to come home, and neither could he.

***

The big day arrived. It's 2016 and we are getting ready to take the three-hour drive to meet my baby at the train station. He made it through! His resilience is shining through the dark clouds that covered his and my life. My son was taken from me through the juvenile court system over fourteen years prior. He had spent his childhood and most of his adulthood behind bars. He was now twenty-eight years old. His little brother was eighteen, and his sister was ten years old. I was forty-seven. Time has moved on. This was a long road for all of us. We visited as often as we could, but that was not the same.

As I write, I still feel sadness because he went through so much. Tyrell told me that although I prayed for him to be acquitted, he believes he had to endure for a purpose. He has said on many occasions that he was headed so far down the wrong road, that had he not been stopped as a youth, he cannot imagine what would have happened. My mom and I were there for Tyrell the entire time. We never stopped believing in him or in God's ability to deliver. But God did not do what we wanted. God did what he knew Tyrell needed. As scripture says, Proverbs 3:5-6 KJV, "Trust in the Lord with all thine heart and lean not unto thine own understanding..." That scripture meant more to me in this situation than ever. I have no idea why my son had to experience this kind of trouble, but I was happy on that glorious day when my son called me with the best news of our lives.

"Momma, I am coming home! I know you never thought I'd do all this time. You had so much faith that I wouldn't, but God knew me better", he said.

"Yes baby, I never thought you'd be gone so long, but God kept you through it all. I know in my heart that this was allowed for something greater. I have held on to that the whole time. I still believe it. You have a testimony son."

"So what time is your train due in and where do I pick you up", I continued in an excited voice.

"It is in Fresno, not far from my grandpa. He wants to be there too", he said joyfully.

My son has always loved his grandpa. He enjoyed visiting him when he was younger. I was excited that Tyrell was coming home, and even more excited that he would be met by his most beloved family members. We were going to be together to welcome him back once he stepped off of the train. The welcome team included his father, in spite of the past, and his little brother, whom he had never met in person. His father and stepmother had him years after they were married. I did not mind coordinating the meet up. I wanted Tyrell to feel all of our love. Before he hung up the phone, he had one more request.

"Oh, Mom, I need some clothes too. I don't have anything but prison clothes."

I replied, "No worries, I will get you something to change into. We will go shopping to get you more. You do not have to worry about a thing."

"Thank you, mo. I love you"

"I love you, too, son."

We hung up. I was excited. I know he was, too. We could not wait for the next few days to pass. He was coming home!

***

The welcoming party showed up for him! Momma, Nana, baby brother, baby sister, his father, his grandfather, and his brother from his dad's previous marriage. He loved family. He missed his own family. As I thought about the trials my son experienced, I just kept seeing that cute little boy, so well-dressed with the fresh haircut, the innocent smile, and those hazel eyes and vanilla skin. He was the product of a milk chocolate momma and a tan daddy, that's that black and brown unity. My son's experience was that of many black and brown teenage males. He got along with all sides and he could be taken as either Hispanic or black, either of which are a targeted group for stereotypical mishandling and misidentification by the politically charged and horrifically managed policing system. The gang database that had been used to identify kids in marked communities played some role in my sons and the sons of many that primed them for the school to prison pipeline. You act up in school you go to continuation school. You meet other troubled youth in those schools and together you feed off of each other, and become even more troubled.

I learned so much from my son's experience. It was important to have male role models and a village to help protect and steer a young black male in the right direction. It is just as important to have a strong system of rehabilitation operating inside the prison, and resources outside to keep the parolee on a progressive path to successful reentry. I do not think there is enough focus on helping the prisoner transition back into society. You hear of many who get out, end up back in, rather quickly. That is because some feel they cannot survive outside of the system to which they have become institutionalized.

Now that my son is home, I am looking forward to helping him to get adjusted to life after prison. That is book he may write himself. The years he has spent in prison allowed him to develop as a writer. He has a book in his belly. He has written poetry, rap lyrics, started a blog page, looking into writing a movie script, and more. I just want to make up for all of the lost years. I want to set him up to win. So, what do I do? I shower him with love. I go all out for his homecoming. I call all of our family and friends to gather and celebrate his return. The feeling is not dissimilar to the story of the prodigal son in the Bible. The father welcomed his son with open arms after he had left the family to do his own thing. I was like that father. As a mom who missed her son terribly, I wanted him to feel loved. I went so far as to "save" Christmas for him! I kept the tree up and left presents under it past December, past January, to February 2016. This was Christmas for my son. Our family was so happy to see him home again. Boy, did we celebrate!

God is so good! It took almost fifteen years. I never thought he'd do the full twelve years he was sentenced, let alone fourteen. I never stopped hoping, praying, believing he would come home. That boy right there has a story to tell! I am still waiting to see the blessing that is to come. Tyrell has been home a while. When he first came home, he enrolled in the local college and took writing classes. He is writing blogs, short stories, and poetry. He has always loved writing. In prison, he wrote enough to produce two novels and possibly a three-hour movie. He really wants to expand into writing music and movie screen plays. Tyrell is truly *resilient*.

# My Poetic Reflection

*That boy right there! Ooh wee! That boy right there, got that smile the swag*
*that look*
*He'll bring you in captivated, oh yeah, you're hooked!*
*Little did you know he's a walking book!*

*That boy right there has a story to tell,*
*One of pain, struggle, survival, my God, he went through hell!*

*There is a great mystery, we don't know why this is his history,*
*But that boy right there he's got the victory,*
*Walking in it, talking in it, speaking his prose through poetry*

*And the light inside energizes his vibe*

*Setting the sparks of his brilliance*
*Showing off his resilience*

*His mother was strong, and grandmother too,*
*They never quit on him; they knew God would bring him through*

*Relentlessly Resilient is how they stand, arm in arm hand in hand*

*Relentlessly trusting that God's Word is true*

*Whatever the reason this family went through so much,*
*What matters is that you will be touched*
*That boy right there has a story to share*

*So, what's his story you ask?*
*Oh, let me tell you it's all about his past.*

*Things he did, wished he didn't, things he live through, while others didn't*

*Y'all just don't know; The hurt, the struggle, the secrets.*
*The way he anesthetized the pain, medicinally to beat this*
*I said medicinally, not medically*

*See, medically prescribed solutions can incapacitate movement or progression,*
*The natural herbal remedy he chose to numb his pain,*
*Would not cause regression, he could proceed in genius perfection*
*He freely flows in thoughts, unchained, no shame.*
*Yeah, pain anesthetized*
*Scribing with the liquid pen, pouring out verses and generating vibes*

*Free-flowing in the LOGOS of Life*
*Scripting the story so folks will retell it right*

*Page 1 to 50 done*

*Keep going... 100, 150, 500 and counting*
*Yeah, it's all coming out pouring, pouring, pouring*
*Done!*

*I am now an open book... read me, learn from me*
*I walked the road your sons glorify, this isn't fantasy*
*They think they can talk trash behind the screen that gives them false security*

*Then they cross paths with the fool they talked crap to last*
*And now their ducking and running to dodge the blast*

*Go ahead, put on them Js, rep your set; show out young bro, chase that clout*
*Beware of the hired hand hiding out, watching and waiting to take you out*

*I took the chances you contemplate.*

*I suffered the consequences you've only heard of,*
*those that can take away your freedom, then you'll be calling hard for the man*
*above*

*Yeah, go ahead and read me*
*I pray you'll stop and think, even cry out loud, if need be*
*Whatever it takes to prevent your momma and granny from asking*
*Why did he have to leave me?*

Writing is a way to heal. It is a vehicle for purging. I am happy to know my son has the gift of writing. I have loved writing since I was in elementary school. My son received that gene as well. Some of the essays he's written are captivating; his blog posts mesmerizing. His time in the system helped develop his talent. He is a father now, along with his younger brother, Jamar. Each of them had sons born to them in 2021. We all went through hell in 2020, but to God be the glory that 2021 has blessed us with a glimpse into the future. What my eldest son went through and my youngest son experienced will not be repeated in the lives of their children. My eldest is already reading books to his baby boy. He keeps audible books playing as well. The next challenge for him is finishing the book he started writing, and focusing on his career. Doing fourteen years in prison is difficult. A person comes out and looks for work, but the criminal record makes it hard for employers to want to hire them. The person has to push and press. He may have to humble himself and take a low wage job just to get in the door.

This can be a hit to the ego and learning to maintain a positive attitude through the rejection is another learning curve. Thank God for organizations that help with ex-offender reentry programs. The struggle is real. Life is hard. Transitioning back is not easy, but do not quit. Tyrell has not quit. He moved in with me for a short while, then reunited with his father and moved back to the Bay area for job opportunities. He found work at a couple of locations, but it is not what he wants to do. He is doing what he has to in order to provide for himself and his new family. He is not making a living as a writer, but will work that in the background. He has a beautiful little boy that needs his dad and mom to be present in his life. My grandson has that. My son puts his son first because of what he went through. I am so proud of him! Tyrell is going to be fine.

## Reflection

*Have you told yourself that life shouldn't be this hard? If you are a Christian, have you wondered where God was when you were going through? Realize this, troubles come and go. The tests get harder, then we learn the lesson, and the easier they become. This is the relentless part of life. It just does not stop. As long as we are focused, we can overcome the resistance and stand in our resilience.*

# Chapter 18

# Load Up! We're Ready for Battle, again!

*There is a time where the battle will not be yours to fight; it is God's.*
*There is also time to put on the whole armor of God, and fight!*

**MJEnvision1t**

I was filled with joy and peace since Tyrell was no longer living his life in prison. I was so excited for him to finally come home and to see him working, exploring his writing talent and going to the local junior college. Those dark days were behind us. I had just bought a beautiful two-story house several months before he came home. I had a patio built, installed a luxury outdoor spa, and had additional concrete installed on one side of the property for a basketball court. My sons and my daughter enjoyed playing ball together. Life was good for us, until trouble came knocking.

I left work one warm spring afternoon in April to head home and start the weekend "See you all Monday", I said to my co-workers. I was glad to be getting off from work and heading to the new house I had just bought. I was living on the nicer side of the Antelope Valley. I headed toward my daughter's school to pick her up from after school care. On my way, I saw a few police cars behind Stater Brothers grocery store just three blocks away from home. There were several guys without shirts sitting on the curb near the police cars. About a city block ahead, I spotted my eldest son riding his bike near my daughter's school. I looked at my watch and saw that my son Tyrell's college class started forty-five minutes ago. I looked to my right, and I saw Jamar's friend, Donathan. As I turned the corner, I saw Tyrell crossing the street on his bike going toward Donathan. I pulled into the parking lot of my daughter's elementary school. I peered toward the street and saw both Tyrell and Donathan pass by. I moved quickly into the school gate toward Kalani's class room. I felt jitters in my stomach and had to get her quickly. Once I signed her out, I told her we had to hurry to the car to get some place quickly. We got to my car as fast as we could. I started the engine and drove out of the parking lot with my one goal, to catch up with Tyrell and Donathan.

When I saw Tyrell, I pulled up to him, rolled down my window and asked why he was not at school. He said he was on his way, but saw Donathan and took a detour. I asked where Jamar was. The look I got from those two boys was disconcerting. I immediately associated the police, the guys on the curb, and my son, Jamar. I panicked. I had no idea what could have happened, but my heart sank. The night before, I had an experience with God. I was praying in my spirit and I received a message that one of my sons was going to be brought down. I shared that with both of my sons that same night. I actually ran down the stairs and into the garage where they were hanging out and I gave them the word from God. I asked them to be careful and think twice about any decisions they were about to make. My sons were not doing anything illegal that I knew of, or could suspect. My middle child was not involved in gangs. My eldest was done with gangs after serving his excessive sentence. My sons did not carry themselves as angry black guys with a chip on their shoulders. They were, however, pretty strong-willed, and would not back down if someone tries to harm them. So, my worry was not that they started any trouble. My worry was that someone came at them, or one of them and something transpired from that. I was getting anxious to know what happened.

"Tyrell, where is Jamar?", I asked worried.

"I don't know mom", Tyrell replied.

"What do you mean you don't know?" I asked.

Since I did not get an answer from Tyrell, I asked Donathan when was the last time he saw Jamar. He said he had not seen him, yet, but Jamar had called earlier saying he was on his way to hang out with him. Jamar never showed up. My heart dropped. I began thinking all kinds of things. I thought he had been shot, was dead, or in jail. I was on a mission to find him. I went looking for him at two other friends' homes and I was surprised at what I saw. I found him outside with a beat-up face, blood on his shirt, and bruised knuckles. I immediately asked, with panic in my voice, "What happened?" He did not want to talk. I offered to take him to the hospital or urgent care, but he did not want to go. I did not know what to do. I had no answers. I offered to take him to his cousin's down in LA to get away for a while. At this point I did not know if folks were going to be looking for him, or what.

So, I drove him to our cousins and he stayed there a few days. In the meantime, I tried to find out what really happened. My son and local weed dealer had gotten into an altercation. My son was childish and made stupid moves at times. He thought he could get the weed and not pay for it, he literally skateboarded away. One guy chased him and began to pummel my son. In order to protect himself, my son grabbed for anything he could find to hit the guy and get him off of him. As soon as he did, three other guys jumped out of a car near the empty field where all of this took place and came for him. The fight was pretty bad, but thankfully no one was shot or killed. Unfortunately, the marijuana dealer was hurt bad enough to have to go to the hospital, and later the police were looking for my son to question him.

Two days later, I heard a knock at my door. It was a police officer. He said he wanted to question Jamar about a matter. Well as a single black mother of black sons, I did not trust the police. I figured I had better get a lawyer before I let them talk to him. So, I stalled until I could. I found a criminal lawyer and retained him, then moved forward. He was a young attorney recommended by someone I trusted. The attorney was a black man, so I felt like he would be able to understand the issues black men have with the criminal justice system, and would help my son navigate the process.

*What a mess.* This lawyer basically just took my money. No real action at all. He had me and my son meet him at the police station to talk to the detective. The point was to do so with a lawyer present. The lawyer never did check to see if there was a warrant out. We arrived, thinking we were there to talk to the detective, but the clerk at the front desk told us to wait a moment and she'd be right back. She came with an officer who was there to put my son in handcuffs. My son was taken into custody. The crooked Sheriffs never responded to any inquiries that this attorney sent. They put an arrest warrant out, and the crappy attorney did not even know. Now, I had to find another lawyer and find bail money. I had just bought my house, did some upgrades, bought a Jacuzzi and put in a patio. Now, I was facing a decision to sell the house to save my son.

*Oh God, why? Why now? Will I ever get out of the cycle of struggling? Why is my son going through this?* I moved out of LA to give him and his sister a better life than what his older brother had, but we are still in this cycle. I know people say you don't question God; you don't ask why. Well, I had to ask. I wanted to know. I needed to understand. I was beginning to feel a lot like Job. As I questioned, the scripture came to me, "...your ways are not my ways, saith the Lord...." Isa 55:8-9.

I asked God, what it was that He was trying to show me, *us?* What was the lesson? *Trust?* Was He teaching me to totally trust in him? I thought I had shown that so many times. I couldn't understand why the potential legal trouble was coming up? I asked when does it stop? I used to feel like I could conquer the world because of my faith and trust in God. In this moment, I was not so sure anymore. I am sure that is how many people feel when the issues of life keep coming to after them, their kids, family, and faith. This is the relentless side of life that refuses to stand down, and when it raises up its ugly head, we have to stand firm against it. This is when you put the armor back on that protects you in spiritual battle.

I had to go back to the scriptures that lifted me when hard times hit. I was going to have to hold up my son. I could not do that if I was not standing strong in my faith. I found that strength and I shared it with him. I told my middle son to trust in God. I told him things would work out. He was scared. He had never been in trouble with the law. I was scared because we lived in a city that is known to throw the book at men and boys of the black and brown persuasion. They are known to have crooked and racist Sheriffs. Jamar's fear was that what if we go all the way to trial and lose? It was self-defense. Why wouldn't he win? Jamar explained that he did not want his fate in the hands of a jury. The Antelope Valley had a reputation for displaying racism against blacks in the area. Therefore, he was afraid they would be biased toward him.

*I could not believe that in 2016, we were having this conversation? We were still dealing with racism in the justice system.*

Jamar was scared. He had another attorney and she advised me to bail him out of jail, quickly. We needed to fight this from outside. We did not want him in jail clothes going to court. Image was and is everything. This was the reality of our justice system. So, I sold the house for quite a bit more than I bought it. I got him out. He was free for the moment, but I wondered if he'd remain free. Life was throwing problems at me left and right. The enemy of my destiny was coming for me by attacking my sons. I was getting a little nervous, but then asked myself, "Where is your trust? Where is your faith?" I started revisiting scriptures from the Bible that addressed worry and anxiety. I began to stand on those by reciting them often. I prayed to God for peace and calm. I never lost faith, although I had moments of wondering when, or how.

As I prayed in my spirit a word came to me that my son would not do prison time. I had a few close prayer warriors stand with me on this. We went through this for several months; preparing for trial, praying, trusting, and believing. The day finally arrived and Jamar had to decide; Jury trial or take a deal? Deals are not always the best choice for men of color. It waves their right to a trial by jury where they have an opportunity to prove their innocence. The problem is that they are trying to prove it to strangers who were not present when the crime was committed.

Strangers are given information; facts and evidence to make a decision over someone's life. Although a jury is supposed to be unbiased, most black men are already guilty before proven innocent by society's standard. My son did not want to take a chance of losing, so he took the deal. He had to accept a charge that was not true. A charge the judge had previously rejected because there was no proof, but the DA packaged the deal with pleading guilty to it anyway. The promise was that he would not go to prison. Well, the cold part about it was that he was stuck with a strike and a felony on his record. He had to do five years on probation. Jamar can be annoying, but he means no harm. Once again, I was dealing with the criminal justice system because of one of my black sons. I moved away from South Central LA to keep the street life away from Jamar. We lived in a nice and clean community with beautiful homes and working-class families, but I could not keep the long arm of the law from tapping on my son's shoulder.

Single parenting was not going well for me with sons. I was a woman of faith, I volunteered in the church and in the community. I stayed engaged with their teachers and supported school programs. I paid tutors to help my kids when they struggled. For the boys to get entangled with police and the court system made no sense to me. I kept looking at myself to see what I was doing wrong. Then I would pray about it. I would feel the Spirit of God telling me there was a purpose, and God will use this situation and your sons to glorify him. I almost felt as if the devil was using my kids to stop the purpose God called me to fulfill. The attacks were so focused and extreme that I could not think of anything else. When I could not make sense of why my sons were going through all of this, I wondered if I was believing a lie about myself. I thought that my calling was to positively impact the lives of young people. I was supposed to lead them to God and out of places of defeat. I was supposed to show them how to develop their talents and discover their purpose. I tried to fulfill this calling through my youth foundation. I tried to fulfill it through fostering. The children that listened and accepted my mentorship have let me know how important I was to them. I was happy to hear that, but my own sons had major struggles. I wanted to see them soar as kids, then teens, and later as men. It did not happen in their childhood, but as men, they're fighting the resistance with small successes.

We made it! Jamar completed the five-year probation sentence. He had never been arrested before. This was a totally out of character situation. He made a childish move and it upset the direction of his young life. Both of my sons were living in society, not locked up. I was happy about that. My middle son struggled to find work due to being on probation and quite a few hours of community service was required. My eldest was released from prison through the parole process and had no trouble finding work, once he moved to the Bay area with his father. It had everything to do with mindset. He was willing to travel outside of his area. He also had plumbing and electric experience from helping his dad with his business. That was one of the benefits of allowing him to live with his father as youth. Most men can teach their sons how to survive by working with their hands, or just by demonstrating what it means to be a provider. My middle son saw me as the provider in our home. He did not experience that from his father. In my world, a college degree gets the job. Having a lot of experience gets the job. He didn't think he could compete. His mindset has been his holdback. He is constantly speaking negatively and ends up sabotaging opportunities that are presented to him. I also realized that I was not helping because I made life very comfortable.

Jamar and his little sister, Kalani were born many years after my first son. By the time they came along, my financial situation was pretty good. That is why I was able to buy my second home when Vernon and I first got married. It is also why I was able to buy my third home in the same city ten years later. I spent time cleaning my credit, getting out of debt, and saving my money in order to recover from the setback after my divorce. I bounced back. My younger children did not know what struggling looked like. They were used to having nice things. Even when I had to go back to food stamps and medi-cal once Vernon and I went our separate ways, my mind was set on rebuilding, and my kids did not feel the financial hit. They were spoiled. I overcompensated with Jamar and Kalani to make up for the loss I experienced with Tyrell and the prison system.

Tyrell tried to talk to his little brother about the importance of working, staying out of trouble, and being responsible. He told him to be appreciative of the people in his life. He shared his trauma stories hoping that his little brother would listen and not make the same mistakes he made. Jamar was not in a gang, but he liked to smoke weed, and play video games, go to the skate park, or play basketball. That was enough for him. Kalani was still young and doing well in school. I was not worried about her like I was Jamar. I had hoped Jamar would learn from his big brother who had so much wisdom to share. Today he and I talk about how his story will change lives. He has the gang experience, he's lived on the streets, slept in his car, fought for his respect in prison, he's had his heart broken by a lady he loved, the list goes on. As I listen to him and as I write, I realize even more that his voice is the faint voice that I heard in the distance. I hear his voice so loud and clear. It is a strong voice and ready to be heard.

# Voice in the Distance

*The voice in the distance was faint, yet loud*
*I heard it in the background, then echoing through the crowd*
*I hate that I couldn't pinpoint it before the crash of misery and pain*
*It was a preventable wreck we should have seen coming*
*I know you are resilient, but I still wish I heard sooner, that voice in the*
*distance.*
*Come on momma, yeah you spoke on it, so no need to dwell on it*
*Yeah, that little boy's life got trauma on it*
*But this man's life got promises on it*
*At birth, the enemy tried to suffocate me,*
*Thank God for your and Nana's prayers*
*They were strong enough to resuscitate me*
*Those prayers kept me from the enemy's snares,*
*Spiritual warfare has been my struggle*
*Hood life? God life? This was hard to juggle*
*I did not know the rules of engagement,*
*So, I lost a few battles, but not the war*
*The full armor of your prayers and even the sword*
*Allowed me to escape through the back door*
*As I ran through the dark wilderness, even down to the pit of hell*
*I had these beautiful black queens, girded up with armor, weapons too*
*Shouting and yelling to sound the alarm and ring the bell*
*We are snatching our boy back from the clutches of hell*
*They used their weapons to do battle for my sanity*
*They refused to let my life be nothing but vanity*
*Surface level stuff; no real substance*
*My Queens were showing me how to overcome the resistance*
*Now like Joseph, I see a vision of me going from the pit to the palace,*
*There would no longer be room for malice*
*Like him, I was caught up, locked up, fed up, and messed up*
*Then a life boat showed up, pulled me out troubled waters*
*and sat me down in silence, giving me time to think*
*about the way things should have been*
*But. I shake it off and smile happily that mercy and grace let me win.*
*The little boys voice you heard in the distance would have forever been silenced*
*but God saw fit to intervene, snatch me up, and sit me down so I could breathe*
*He whispered to me "I know the plans I have for you…"*
*My journey was and is my journey, momma, you planted good seed,*
*The harvest is here.*

## Reflection

*How many times have you reflected back on your life and realized something that was always there in your life? Or realized that there was a plan for your life all along and only at this age, or this point did you realize it is so? Think on the scripture that says, "I know the plans I have for you, declares the Lord. Plans to prosper you and not to harm you, plans to give you a future and a hope. Jeremiah 29:11*

# Chapter 19

# Unexpected Stranger My Catalyst for the Big Change

*Some people are in your life to help you along your journey to purpose. You are not always meant to build a long-lasting relationship. Activate your sense of discernment and pay attention to those who God has allowed in your life for an appointed time, and only for that time.*

MJEnvision1t

*Can I Love Again?* After all of the drama, the lies, and the headaches I experienced in relationships all while dealing with my sons, I was not interested in dating. I had been single most of my life. I rarely allowed new men in. If I wanted to go out, I'd just go with someone I already knew from the past. So, when this younger man I met at work started flirting with me, I was quick to turn my attention elsewhere. He was persistent, though. He was young, just seven years older than my eldest son and he had his eyes on me. Young man, older woman, uh no! Never crossed my mind before. No, I am not a cougar. I just happen to look very young for my age. That is why Tyler had no problem approaching me and asking for my number. I wasn't interested, initially. However, his charm, his swag, and his intellect had me hooked before I knew it.

We met while soaring through the southern California sky on a sunny day, enjoying the view, and chatting with my co-workers. I didn't notice the man who sat behind me on the plane had been checking me out the whole time. I was on business travel on Halloween 2018. Just a day trip to a beautiful golf resort in one of California's most sought-after communities in San Diego. As we exited the plane and awaited the company shuttle, I continued talking to my co-workers. The shuttle pulled up and we stepped inside. I heard a man talking to the shuttle driver about the pickup schedule. I looked over to see who was talking and I noticed a tall, professionally dressed man who I had never seen at work before. I turned back to continue my conversation, and thought nothing else of the guy.

The day went on, our business team had a wonderful breakfast in a restaurant located on the golf course, with beautiful views of the greens. We strategized plans for the upcoming new year, and shared what we learned over the past ten months. Since it was Halloween, we decided to dress up in a costume and take pictures. Actually, we photo shopped the pictures. One of the managers who met us at the San Diego site was dressed in an emoji costume. We took turns wearing it, took pictures, then merged our photos. We did a good job, if I may say so myself. Back to the story of the man on the plane. After we completed our offsite manager's meeting, we headed back to the office to await the shuttle. The well-dressed man from the plane was standing out in front of the building waiting. I was also there, but was talking to one of the other managers. The man from the plane interrupted my conversation.

"Excuse me," he said, "Do you know if this is where the shuttle is going to pick us up?"

"Yes, I responded. It should be here in about 15 minutes."

"Oh okay, thank you." He replied, then continued, "I did not want to stand here waiting only to find out I am in the wrong location."

"I understand," I replied, then turned back to continue my conversation with my co-workers, but my manager had walked up and had engaged James in a different conversation. The unexpected stranger approached me again.

"Excuse me, I did not get your name…"

"It's Nikki,"

"Nikki, it is nice to meet you, I am Tyler."

"Hello Tyler. Were you here for a meeting, too?" I asked.

Tyler replied that he was there for an interview. I asked how it went and told me that he believed it went well. Before he continued, the shuttle arrived and we boarded. I sat toward the middle, so I could finish a conversation with my co-worker. I happened to turn my head slightly and saw that Tyler had sat just across from me. I was not expecting that. Tyler asked me questions about what I do and then shared what he does. He explained the job he had interviewed for and why he was looking at other opportunities. I cut the conversation short so that I could engage with my co-workers. We arrived at the airport, and took our seats in the lounge until our private plane arrived. Tyler sat right next to me, again and started talking to me. At some point he told me his birthday was coming up and that he would be thirty-seven. I told him I had a son who would be thirty-one, and a daughter whose birthday was the same day as his. *Interesting.* Obviously, I was much older and there was no way this man would want to continue the conversation. I was wrong. The conversation continued. We talked the entire time on the 50-minute flight back to the Antelope Valley.

I wondered where this conversation was going. This guy knew how old I was by now, but he was still talking to me. Maybe he just likes to talk. I don't know. When we exited the plane, he asked me for my last name so he can look me up and message me at work. I told him. Monday, morning, I logged on to my computer, opened my email, and saw a message from Tyler. *Hey it was nice meeting you. I am just keeping in touch. Have a nice day.*

Uh oh! *What was happening here? Is he interested in me?* We had a huge age difference. I did not think I should even try to see where it could go? *Girl, folks are going to call you a cougar if you end up going out with this guy.* I told myself to stop thinking about it. It may not be anything. Well, I could not focus on work, so I decided to send him an instant message saying, "hey, I got your email, you have a nice day, too". Tyler replied and asked for my phone number. I hesitated, then went ahead and gave it to him. He called me. He had this deep night time DJ soulful voice. I was getting pulled in by his magnetic personality. I asked him if he had heard back from the interview. He told me that he was still waiting, and then proceeded to tell me he had other interviews lined up. I let him know that I had to get back to work, but wanted to continue the conversation. I asked him out for coffee at Starbucks. He accepted the invitation.

"Hi, Tyler!" I said with a smile.

"Hey, how are you?" He replied.

"I am good, thanks." I responded with a little smirk on my face

"What would you like me to get you?" He asked.

"I'll take a tall Iced Chai tea latte". I replied, then got us a table and waited.

Tyler walked over with our iced drinks, took a seat, and began talking to me about the flight we met on. Tyler is smart and a polished professional, and I liked that about him. It was a welcomed change. I have had a hard time in my relationships as a result of my drive, go-getter personality, and disenchantment with men who did not want more out of life. I started desiring men who were in leadership roles on their jobs, who worked out regularly, liked to travel, and enjoyed going out to dinner, concerts, and enjoyed golfing. *Yes, I said it, golfing!* I had been with bad boys most of my life and I was tired of the outcome. I wanted someone on my level or higher. Tyler fit the image, but he was so freaking young. *Why? Why did I meet him that day and why did he reach out to me? Even more, why did I respond to him? What was I thinking?*

Tyler and I made plans to meet the following day at Applebee's. I was a little nervous to see him in this setting and in the evening, but I was open to trying the dating thing since I had been out of the game for a long time. We had a couple of drinks, and ate pretty well. We talked a lot. We had so much to say. At the end of the date, Tyler walked me to my car, then hugged me. His tall, thick, muscular body made me feel so secure. I did not want him to let go. Then, he bent down toward me, and pressed his lips against mine. It was over! His kiss was like none other. It was so passionate, yet gentle. No man had ever made me feel that good from a kiss. What in the world was going on? *He was 13 years younger than me. He was looking for job opportunities away from here, we will not have a chance. Just back off of this. Don't go any further. This is not going to turn into anything.* Those were thoughts running through my mind.

"Ok Tyler, well I better get home. I had a nice time."

"Yeah, me too. I will talk to you tomorrow."

"Okay. Good night."

I sat in my car and asked myself if I was ready to involve myself with someone new? I had been so used to just dealing with men from my past. Men who I already knew well. I knew their ways, their habits, the good and the bad. If I get involved with Tyler, I would have to get to know him. I had no history with him. Did I really want to go through that? Did I want to put that kind of time in? Before I knew it, I was already moving forward with Tyler. He actually moved on me pretty quickly. We started talking every day about everything you can think of. We talked politics, relationships, religion, parenting, goals, travel, you name it. He was an open book, and I was not used to that from men. Tyler became very transparent with me about his life, his family, and issues he had been dealing with. He allowed himself to be vulnerable to me. I have not experienced this with a man. They were always keeping secrets. They were not forthcoming with anything. Tyler trusted me with information about himself. I liked that. Maybe this could work.

"Hey, what are you doing this weekend?" Tyler asked me.

"I am preparing a presentation for work on Monday", I responded.

"Oh, I wanted to know if you would go with me to Santa Barbara Sunday and stay over since I have an interview Monday."

"Oh, that sounds nice. I wish I could." I said.

"It's okay. I understand." He replied.

I was experiencing treatment I had not had before, except with Kevin. Kevin and did not work out although we tried a couple of times. To this day, he is still my best friend forever. We are just better that way. Tyler was turning out to be someone I could enjoy hanging out with. He had shared his hurts, his desires, and his concerns. I shared my faith and trust in God to help me through my struggles. Tyler had been so open to hearing about God. This was another positive for this guy. A man who wants God in his life. A man who was open to hearing what I have to say about God and faith? This was going in the right direction. We started watching TD Jakes on Facebook live together. I would log on and I would see the pop up "Tyler is watching with you." That made me smile. We would later talk about the sermon and share what it meant to us.

Tyler asked if I had plans for Christmas break; our job shuts down for the holidays. I told him I was just hanging with family. He told me he was going to spend the whole time with me and my family. *What? A man who is telling me he is going to be with me during the holidays? Well I'll be... This is it! This has got to be the one. Thank you, Jesus!*

Anytime he called, I would come running. He'd call me about an hour after I had gotten home from work and ask what I was doing. I would tell him I was heading out to the gym. He'd immediately tell me I was not, but instead I needed to be headed to meet him for breakfast. I'd say no and make excuses, but he had a way of convincing me to change my plans.

We spent a lot of time talking about our relationship with God; to the point where we felt like God put us together. He told me how he was almost an atheist when we met, but I brought him back to God. Today, he leans on God to help him through his challenges. He gives God the credit for the big changes in his life. Although we openly professed our love for God, we were fornicating. I call it what it is, sin is sin. We did not exercise self-control over our flesh. The passion between us was so strong. We prayed together and even shared sermons from you tube. We thought we were supposed to be together. God help us!

Tyler had received the call he had been waiting for. The opportunity to make more money, get back on his feet, and get his son back home with him. He called to tell me that he had the offer from a major aerospace company in Dallas, TX. He told me he was probably going to take it. Tyler was a quite worldly person who loved being in the action. He was a drinker, he loved fast cars, rubbing shoulders with big shots at work, and had to have the best living quarters and the hottest car. I remember him saying, he needed to make changes in his life. He was tired of the struggle. He was sharing a place with a roommate. He did not like the city he was working and living in, mostly because it was far away from all the action, and as he said, the Antelope Valley didn't even have a Whole Foods! He lived in Beverly Hills for a little while before moving to our community. As a child, he and his mom lived on a country club, so he was used to a high-end lifestyle.

Well, I understand the Antelope Valley didn't offer the lifestyle he was used to. So, I told him to do what he had to do. I remember the conversation so well. I told Tyler I would miss him, but I get it. He had to do what was best for himself. I really liked him, and we spent good times together. Tyler let me know that he enjoyed spending time with me too. He was a little concerned about leaving me and leaving his new friends, those he called his "boys" in the AV. He began ranting a little about how there are no guarantees with people; they come and go. There was no guarantee that his friends that he called his "boys" would even stay. They may get a new opportunity and leave, or I may decide I didn't want to be with him. I told him since he had so many reasons to go, he should go. He asked me to consider leaving the Antelope Valley. I was open to it. I just wasn't going to do it for him. I had a lot to consider, especially my daughter. I also had my sons, even though Tyrell was older, he was still navigating life after prison. Jamar was treading water with trying to stay out of trouble while on his five-year journey through probation. I was not sure what I wanted to do. I was getting tired of Jamar not rising to his full potential. I was beginning to wonder if I was handicapping him. He was so dependent on me. I had to think hard about my next move. What would be in it for me?

Although Tyler said he understood that I would not move just for him, he did not let up on trying to convince me. He called and asked when I was going to visit. I was like really? Are you sure you want me out there with you? He said yes, he really did. So, I set up a couple of interviews, booked my flight and ultimately made it to Dallas the week of Valentine's Day.

When I arrived, Tyler picked me up from the airport, actually valet, as is always his style. No dealing with pick up lines in front of the airport baggage claim area. We went out to eat, Tyler seemed excited to see me, but the next day was Valentine's Day and he was different. Not as passionate as he had been. Distant, almost as if he did not want me there. He got upset at the smallest thing I said, then blamed me for it. I knew something was not, right? I thought maybe he met someone, and did not know how to tell me. Maybe he was second guessing us since I was so much older. I went ahead and asked him straight out what was going on. He told me he couldn't do this anymore. He did not know if he wanted to be in a relationship. He had too many issues he was dealing with.

I said to him, "Okay, Tyler. I get it. I prefer you to be honest about your feelings. We are friends if nothing else, and I am not easily broken. It hurts, but I will be okay. I want you to be okay. He hugged me and we both cried in each other's arms and ultimately fell asleep. We kissed good bye in the morning, and I went home thinking we were done.

Lo and behold! The phone rings. It's Tyler "hey what are you doing…" Oh boy, here we go again. I was about to get back on a roller coaster ride. He was missing me and not sure what he wanted to do about it. I thank God that I was older than him and had years of experiences with men and life in general. It was so easy for me to keep emotions out of sound decision-making, by this time. I told him I was actually going to make the move. I was doing it for me and not for him. So, I did. It was the best move of my life, even though there were significant bumps in the road. The journey was a rough one, but I made it through. Tyler had issues he had to work out, but he'd project them on me. He was trying to figure himself out. It wasn't enough that he made very good money, lived in a highly sought-after neighborhood in Dallas, and drove Hellcat! He was always seeking more. Kind of like me. I realized that he was not the man for me. I needed someone who loved God and allowed God to lead him so he can in turn, lead his family. Tyler was not there yet.

Yes, I am here now living my new life in Texas. Living my best life. Excited I am in a new church home. I am in a middle-class community; in an excellent school district for my daughter. I make very good money. I am happy. What else could I want? Marriage is not it. I have a problem in keeping relationships. My tolerance level is low for any man who is immature, insecure, or doesn't show enough interest in me. I have the attitude that I'd rather be alone than to deal with your drama. My relationship with Tyler was ok as long as we didn't see too much of each other. I liked it that way. I was really getting closer in my relationship with God. I was rethinking why I was dealing with Tyler. Initially I felt like God brought us together. Later, the disagreements and not paying enough attention to me, yet wanting all the attention on himself, was getting to me. The miscommunication between us; one thinking that the other is trying to hurt the other with words, and the other oblivious. He would say, "But that's not really what happened it's just you thinking that way. You know how it goes." I was beginning to question the relationship. Not the decision to move.

I did pray to the Lord to open up doors of opportunities for me to get into project management and that is exactly what happened. It happened for me in Texas. A place where the cost-of-living was amazing and I was able to bring my California salary. So, I really believed my steps were ordered by God. He did use Tyler as a catalyst for me to make this mov, but that did not mean that he planned for Tyler and I to be a couple, and happily married for the rest of our lives. When you know who you are and are focused on a mission, a dream, a vision, a goal; you will not allow another person to take that fire from you. Tyler began to do that to me. He was draining my energy because he needed me to pour into him and he could not reciprocate. It is my prayer that women and men will develop an inner strength that they can draw from when they find themselves stuck in a situation that is not aligned to their purpose. It's okay to let people go. It hurts, but time will heal the pain.

## Reflection

*Who or what is draining your energy? Is anyone or anything keeping you from your purpose? Sometimes distractions come subtly, even in disguise. They are a part of what I call the resistance. Their purpose is to stop you from meeting goals, and ultimately, hinder you from operating in your purpose.*

# Chapter 20

# Taking those Ls with Grace

*When things go great, watch out, that devil ain't never happy. He will come at you with some stuff to knock you off your high horse. But guess what. If he knocks you off, get back up, swinging!!!!*

**MJEnvision1t**

I had quite a few wins, and quite a few losses. I will tell you, though, I took those Ls with grace! That's being *resilient*. All of the trials and situations I shared with you has shaped the way I look at, and respond to life. I sum it up to a test of faith. I don't have any clue why our Creator would want to do such a thing, but it is what it is; a faith test. If you pass it, life looks so much better on the *other* side of it. If you fail, life keeps looking bad on the *same* side of it. You actually stay in a slump, a rut, if you will, because you are not learning and growing from the trials. You are living in a wilderness, or valley and can't seem to find your way out, or up the mountain. Every situation I have been through, I've learned from. I've asked God what it is he wanted me to learn, then I waited for the answer. I have found that I move from glory to glory as a result. My roller coaster ride from welfare, to homeowner, from homeowner to food stamps, from food stamps to another home, from that home to renting again, and from renting again to planning my next purchase developed my faith on the financial side of things. The relational side of my learning spectrum went from happy with my boyfriend to single with a baby, then back in a relationship, and single with a baby, then married, divorced, and single with a baby. I learned how to trust in God to take care of me and my children.

On the spiritual side, I went from being taught through Catholicism, then Pentecostal, Baptist, Episcopal, and finally non-denominational. From this, I learned that my relationship with God the Father is just that; my relationship. Career-wise, I went from fast food, to retail, to accounting office clerk, to budget analyst, financial planner, cost manager, and today project manager. I love where I am and what I have learned in my career. I am sure you, who's reading this book, have a similar journey. These are transitions, or even milestones of life. We all go through problems, face obstacles, or get lost for a moment, and even hide out from time-to-time. The difference between those who get stuck and stay stuck is how much they believe they can overcome. It is all in how we think. Life's consequences are based on our decisions. Our decisions and actions are based on our thoughts. Our frames of reference play a part in how we make our decisions. How big or how small your faith is, determines how much you will pour into overcoming a challenge.

Trials, challenges, and obstacles do not stop, unfortunately. These things are what I call *"the resistance."* Overcoming the resistance is challenging, but should be your goal and it is certainly mine. It is important to build up your mind in order to effectively handle what life throws at you. I thought I had finally made it. I made a huge decision to let my boys become men. I made the choice to leave California and come to Texas for financial betterment and quality of life. I let them stay in the house I was renting, but they were responsible for the paying the rent now. For a few months, things were great. I was able to save nearly $1000 per month since I did not have to pay the high state tax that California required. I no longer had to pay those high gas prices to fill up my car. My job was less than 10 miles away. My luxury apartment was amazing! The glistening pool view from my balcony made me feel like I was living in a resort. The guy I was seeing was showing me a life I had not experienced before with a man. He took me to fancy restaurants in downtown Dallas. We toured the area and checked out the view of the city from the top of Reunion Tower. This was the high life. Although I did not need all of that, I started to enjoy it because this lifestyle was presented to me by a man, I was not treating myself, I was not paying for the meals anymore, he was. I am here in Texas living my best life! Making money, saving money. Paying off bills. Loving my new church, my new role at work. I am able to help my kids get on their feet.

Challenges are many; victories are few. Not to say that challenges outweigh the victory; by no means. Often times, we go through so much just to get a victory, that it feels as if they are few and far between. As you know, when things go great, watch out, that devil ain't never happy. He will come at you with some stuff to knock you off your high horse. But guess what. If he knocks you off, get back up, swinging!!!! I was diagnosed with breast cancer two weeks before the stay-at-home orders and a mask mandate was issued due to the COVID 19 worldwide pandemic. The day my doctor called me with the diagnosis, I was at work. I took the call from my doctor, got up from my desk and stepped out of the office. I stood in the hallway and listened. I had been preparing for good news. I was in prayer and reading the Word of God. I was not shaken. I kept myself covered in prayer. I took it like a champ. I was told it was caught early and can be taken out surgically. I had been through so many trials that my faith had been built up. I was prepared for this next attack and did not realize it. I was not too worried when the doctor said surgery would take care of it. My attitude was, ok, it's time to see the surgeon.

I drove up to the Texas Breast Center and I waited to see the doctor, mask and all. I pray always, but I will admit I was a little concerned about being in the medical office with this virus all over the place. A nurse called me in from the lobby. She took my vitals, asked a few questions, then told me the doctor would be in shortly. I did not wait long, before the breast surgeon opened the door and introduced herself. I met Dr. Seda.

"Hello Monique. How are you?" She asked.

"I feel great, thank God!" I said in a positive voice.

"I have some good news for you," she said. "The type of breast cancer you have is hormone positive and it is in its very early stage. This means we can slow the growth with hormone blockers until we can schedule surgery."

I asked, so when would the surgery take place. She let me know that because of the pandemic, they could not do any surgeries unless they were considered urgent. Although it was cancer, it was not an aggressive form.

"I responded; well Praise be to God for that!" I had a little more time to decide which surgery I wanted; lumpectomy, mastectomy or double mastectomy. I agreed to meet with the oncologist to start taking the hormone blockers. I learned later these can cause blood clots. I began to worry about that. So much for my faith, right? Not so fast, I did get nervous about the pills, but I did not hang out in my worry. I went into my prayer closet. This is something I started doing after watching the movie the War Room, for the second time. I asked for wisdom, and afterward, I awaited an answer. For me the answer was clarity and confidence in my decision to take it or not to take it. I decided not to and asked for an alternative. I got it.

The year 2020 was a major test of my faith and resiliency. Real hard life situations hit. They hit me and you; they hit the world. The attack of the enemy was extremely strong. Three months into the new year and I was hit with personal bad news while the world was being hit with tragedy after tragedy. From January 2020 to May 2020, it was all bad. The GOAT! Kobe Bryant was killed in a helicopter crash with his daughter Gigi, her friend, and coaches from her basketball team were the first in a series of bad news. That was devastating. He was a legend. He was young. He had just retired from basketball. He had just gotten a Grammy for a book he wrote. Who would have thought this man's life would be cut off that short along with his daughter. She was an aspiring young basketball player. That was at the last week of January, 2020. The last week of February, 2020, I was diagnosed with breast cancer, and after that, the third week of March 2020, the world was in a pandemic!

The world was shut down. Commerce halted. Many began to work from home. We wore masks and gloves, used hand sanitizer everywhere. The pillage in the stores was so bad that we could barely get toilet paper. Eventually, we adjusted to the shortage of supplies, the mask mandate, and stay at home orders, but that also came to an end with the senseless murder of another black man. This happened in May of 2020! Oh, we must back up to April! Vigilantes took the life of a young black male jogger. We had just come out of the year 2019 enjoying a time where life seemed to be going so well. Yet, suddenly it all paused. The world just stopped. *Was my peace and happiness under false pretenses? Was I delusional about my life's purpose, or about the power of my faith? What was I thinking, posting things on social media like, I am blessed? Or, telling friends how God has ordered my steps? What was I doing looking forward to getting active in my new church home? What was I doing taking classes to discover my purpose?* I had been in search of my purpose for as long as I can remember? I am supposed to be speaking to large groups and to individuals about faith and trust in God. I was supposed to be helping them to discover their purpose, you know the saying, "each one, teach one". How is this going to happen when the world has been turned upside down?

The real faith test started in 2020. The question became *where do we go from here?* Do we just adapt to a new lifestyle of working from home, staying inside, and wearing masks when we go out? Or how about this, do we totally rely and trust in God that we will be safe because we are covered by the blood of Jesus? Do we declare that no weapon that is formed against us will prosper? Do we go out in public believing that we shall live and not die? Should we shout that He filled us with the Holy Spirit and no plague shall harm us? What happens if we don't take this position as Christians? Are we walking in fear and not faith? The battle of the mind is real. Faith over fear! Declare it! That's what I have been hearing more and more; from the pulpit to Facebook posts, people have begun offering advice on how to prepare for this next faith journey.

I've received nutritional books on how to naturally heal cancer and how to avoid Covid 19. I've had friends in my ear, reminding me to go to the Lord and ask for His guidance, wisdom, and his protection; to claim my victory. All of the teachings over my lifetime that were swirling around in my head telling me to declare the Word of God. Telling me *I am victorious, or I am more than a conqueror.* Others began to surface in my head; *with long life will I satisfy you, you shall live and not die, for the Lord God heals all of your diseases.* And yet, I felt some sense of nervousness, worry, and doubt. As these feelings of nervousness and anxiety came to mind, I quietly sat on the end of my bed, picked up my cell phone, and started searching scriptures to meditate on. I read Philippians 4:6 to get my mind settled and I was good. I chose peace. I chose it in my mind and in my home. If I have learned nothing else in my growth and journey as a Christian woman, I have learned this from the teachings of my Savior, Jesus the Christ, Yeshua Hamashiach, and that is the Kingdom of Heaven suffers violence and the violent take it by force (Matthew 11:12, KJV).

Well guess what? I am taking Heaven by force! I am doing spiritual warfare against any enemy that has been assigned to attack, defeat, demolish, or to destroy me. I stand covered by the blood of Jesus. I stand with the Holy Spirit residing in me! I stand with angels beside me going into battle against the enemy who seeks to destroy me, and those connected to me! I know that I win, we win, because the Word of God tells me that God wins. I am a follower of God the Father and a follower of Jesus the Christ. I operate under the power of the Holy Spirit and I declare Isa 54:17 (KJV) that *no weapon formed against me will prosper.* So, I pull up my bootstraps, so to speak, and I get ready to win my battle. All praise be to Jehovah! All honor be to the Lord Yeshua Hamashiach. I now understand what it means to fight a spiritual battle; to do spiritual war fare. People think that our issues are strictly in the physical realm. They think that the person who upset them is the problem. They blame the lack of money or sickness as the issue or obstacle. They don't realize that the mindset is the real issue. We must change our mindset in order to handle these situations when they arise. We must renew our minds as the Bible says in the Book of Romans. These earthly issues don't matter when you tap into the higher things of God.

This is what Jesus taught and why the leaders of that day rejected him. They could not understand how a man in the flesh could speak to and operate under the spiritual might and power of God. They questioned his authority. Jesus thought from a whole different level, a different planet, if you will. The religious people were angry because he was upsetting their current way of living, thinking, and believing. They didn't want anything to upset their traditions. They were trapped in religion. I praise God, that although I am a Christian, and that is considered a religion, I don't see it that way. I see it as a relationship with God the Father, and made possible by my savior Jesus the Christ. I really believe that the man Jesus, the Son of God Jesus, and the Holy Spirit that Jesus left on this earth, was sent from God to show us how to connect with God the Father in the heavenly realm. The Word of God tells us that we need to think on heavenly things and know that God will take care of us. Jesus was teaching us to have total reliance and dependence on God the Father. This is not to say that we are to be walking around in *"la la land"* without a care in the world, living in total denial. It is an admonishment to change the way we think about our situations, so that we can excel and not become defeated. To do this, we must operate in Holy Spirit power. This is the power that enables us to overcome that which has been resisting our ability to achieve the promises of God.

I praise God for Jesus who taught the people of the land what faith looks like in action. I am thankful for the scribes of that time who captured the experiences of those who believed and put that information in the Word of God. The Word is for us to apply to our lives. We need to hear the Word before we can become doers of the Word. Hearing how God's Word heals, saves, creates, builds, gives us a foundation from which to build our faith. Faith is more than belief; it is acting on the belief. As scripture tells us, faith without works is dead, James 2:14-26. If you do not have faith to overcome that which is resisting you, or if you do not believe in the power of God to restore you, you are keeping yourself from experiencing great resilience.

Jesus explained that He would be going back to the Father, but would leave His Holy Spirit in the earth. Because Jesus went back to the Father, the Holy Spirit was made available to us for empowerment. Jesus said we would have power to do the things that He did an even greater, when the Holy Spirit comes upon us, Acts 1:8 (KJV). Once I got this into my spirit, I started realizing that I am defeated only if I allow myself to be. I can overcome the resistance if

I operate under the power of His Holy Spirit. I pondered my faith, then I realized who I am and that I really am here on purpose. I answered my own question; Am I delusional? *No, I am not.* My peace and happiness are not based on how life is going. It is not based on situations. If that were the true, I would be a nut case! It is based on my level of trust in God. I have come to trust Him during my battles, even when I don't see Him in them. The battles have been preparing me for such a time as this. I am ready for the next level God has for me. I suffered like many others, but my relentless desire to achieve and discover purpose was the perfect ingredient for *my relentless resilience.*

My story is not finished by any means. I believe there is much more to come, but I'm on another level now. I'm not perfect, that status belongs to Jesus. I'm human and as long as I'm in this human body I'm going to be limited. We all are. I'm working towards being limitless in my belief system. Limitless in Kingdom thinking. I'm so thankful that God has surrounded me with people who are Kingdom minded. These are the *Relentless* ones. Those who keep getting up after being hit with an issue of life. I'm learning from others about their journey out of the valley of discouragement and disappointment to the mountain of joy and peace that no human can understand. I have experienced that peace quite a few times while in the midst of a storm, and it feels good.

There is someone out there who can heal or learn for what I have gone through, or what my sons have dealt with. It is my prayer that this book has ministered to you by showing you that peace is your decision. You can decide to be at peace in the midst of your storms. Once you decide to be at peace. Let go of the situation and turn it over to Jesus. Praise Him for every trial, because He will get the Glory as you come out of it. When he gets the glory, his glory rains down on you and you share in that glorious moment with him. As the Bible says, we are joint heirs with Jesus the Christ, so why don't we take our places in the kingdom, and live life with a joy that surpasses all understanding? Embracing this idea is embracing the fact that you are *Relentlessly Resilient.*

# Bibliography

1. *What to Do When Your Children Blame You for Your Divorce (weinbergerlawgroup.com)*

2. *Punishment for Profit: The Economics of Mass Incarceration, Joyce Chediac, May 4, 2015 www.workers.org/2015/05/19812).*

3. *Battlefield of the Mind: Winning the Battle in Your Mind, Joyce Meyer1995*

Made in the USA
Middletown, DE
18 October 2022